To our "boys"

    Roger and Jake

    Douglas, Adam, and Dylan

Who truly support us, love us, and give us the time to grow!

Thoroughly Fit

Becky Tirabassi
& Candice Copeland-Brooks

ZondervanPublishingHouse

Grand Rapids, Michigan

A Division of HarperCollinsPublishers

Requests for information should be directed to:
Zondervan Publishing House
Grand Rapids, Michigan 49530

ISBN 0-310-40301-4

All Scripture quotations, unless otherwise noted, are taken from the *Holy Bible: New International Version* (North American Edition). Copyright © 1973, 1978, 1984, by the International Bible Society. Used by permission of Zondervan Bible Publishers.

Edited by Lori J. Walburg
Cover design by Cheryl Van Andel
Interior design by Jack Rogers
Interior illustrations by Paul Montgomery
Cover photography:
 © 1993 COMSTOCK, INC/Mike and Carol Werner
 © 1993 COMSTOCK, INC
 Jon Gundry
 Steven Harvey
 Stuart Schulze Photography

Printed in the United States of America

CONTENTS

INTRODUCTION

❖❖

*C*andice and I [Becky] first met over the telephone when I called her to discuss the possibility of working together on a fitness video. Over the next year and a half, as we worked on *Step Into Fitness*, we discovered that we had a lot in common as wives and moms who also work outside of the home as writers and motivators. As our friendship grew, we often shared our struggles to lead that elusive balanced life.

The more we talked about these issues, the more we realized that many people were looking for:

❖ a healthy lifestyle that challenges us mentally and physically,
❖ the happiness that comes from loving your family and friends, and
❖ the hope and peace that fill your life when God is at its center.

We came to realize that if all four areas—physical, mental, emotional, and spiritual—were balanced, we'd be *thoroughly fit!*

Our hope—and purpose—in writing this motivational devotional is to give you creative and practical tools that will inspire you to make significant lifestyle changes. Because we've all witnessed the failure of the "quick fix" approach to change, the goal of *Thoroughly Fit* is to encourage you, day by day, one step at a time, to make changes that will become a permanent part of your life.

Each day we have chosen a positive thought to inspire and motivate you. Next, we offer practical tips and current information in all four lifestyle areas and allow you to chart your course. Finally, we close each day's devotional with "Prayers & Passages," which gives you the opportunity to meditate on a portion of Scripture and to pray.

We would also like to encourage you to check into the companion step aerobic videos, *Step Into Fitness* and *Thoroughly Fit*. Each video contains 70 minutes of fun and challenging step aerobics choreographed to well-known Christian contemporary songs. These are safe, balanced, low-impact workouts that will burn calories and body fat. Suitable for beginning through advanced level steppers, the videos will give you a great aerobic, leg, and abdominal workout, as well as condition your upper body. The results? You'll not only trim your fat and improve your cardiovascular system and your muscle tone— but you'll also be one step closer to achieving the physical goals you have set for yourself!

As you go through this 90-day journey, you will focus on:
❖ Setting goals
❖ Getting and staying motivated
❖ Planning ahead, and
❖ Celebrating your achievements

Are you ready?

PART ONE:

Goals

✦ ✦
✦ ✦
✦ ✦
✦ ✦
✦ ✦

*A goal is something you
intend to do or achieve.
The purpose of this section
is to help you focus on your
strengths, set personal
goals, and grow in three
areas: self-awareness,
self-acceptance,
and self-care.*

Self-awareness

✦ ✦

✦ ✦

✦ ✦

This 90-day journey begins by helping you become aware of who you are, what you like to do, and what you are doing now. During this week we will set long-term, short-term, and daily goals. You will individualize your goals by discovering your likes and dislikes, wants and needs. At the end of this week, you will schedule your new priorities into your lifestyle.

Each day will include a motivational quote, practical tips, an inspirational Scripture passage, a prayer, and a place to record your thoughts, prayers, and progress.

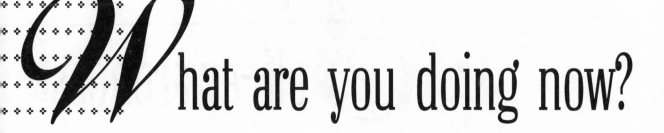

What are you doing now?

Positive Thought

You cannot plough a field by turning it over in your mind.

Anonymous

Practical Tip ✦

Becoming more conscious of your physical movement is the first step toward a more active lifestyle.

The following worksheet will help you assess your current level of activity and recognize when you're the most active and when you're the least active. In a few weeks, you will return to this same chart to reassess your activity level.

For each two-hour block of the day, determine what you are usually doing. Use the activity level guide and rate that time slot as a "low," "medium," or "high" activity level. For each low activity level block, give yourself one point. Medium activity level blocks will receive two points, and high activity level blocks will receive three points. Total your points, but more importantly, be aware of what your overall activity level is right now.

Activity Level Guide

Low: Sedentary or little activity
- ❖ sleeping
- ❖ watching TV
- ❖ driving
- ❖ reading/studying

Medium: Busy around home or work
- ❖ housework/shopping
- ❖ gardening
- ❖ moving around office
- ❖ running errands

High: Vigorous activity or exercise
- ❖ brisk walking
- ❖ any sport or aerobic activity that is vigorous for at least 15 minutes at a time

	LOW	MEDIUM	HIGH
6am–8am			
8am–10am			
10am–12pm			
12pm–2pm			
2pm–4pm			
4pm–6pm			
6pm–8pm			
8pm–10pm			

Totals: _____   _____   _____

- ❑ I feel good about my activity level.
- ❑ I would like to make a few changes in my activity level.
- ❑ I absolutely need to make changes in my activity level.

Prayers & Passages

Give ear to my words, O LORD, consider my sighing. Listen to my cry for help, my king and my God, for to you I pray. In the morning, O LORD, you hear my voice; in the morning I lay my requests before you and wait in expectation.

Psalm 5:1–3

As I begin my 90-day journey, Lord, I realize that I cannot change certain things about my past or what body type I have inherited. But with your help, I *can* make changes that are practical, possible, and pertinent. Please show me how to make those changes—on Day 1, Day 90, and every day. I invite you to walk with me each day of this journey and to be my guide. Please give me courage and grant me strength. Amen.

What do you like to do?

Positive Thought

Sitting still and wishing makes no person great. The good Lord sends the fishing, but you have to dig the bait.

Anonymous

Practical Tip

Finding activities that you like to do is one of the keys to developing a more active lifestyle. Remember, a busy life is not necessarily an active life. By identifying activities that you like to do now, or would like to try as part of your lifestyle change, you will move forward into your goal-setting days with purpose.

Answer the following questions regarding your personal preferences in each of these areas:

WHERE would you like to be active?
    Outdoors_____
    Indoors at home_____
    At a health club or gym_____

WHEN would you like to be active?
    Early morning_____
    Mid-morning_____
    Afternoon_____
    Evening_____

WHAT types of activities do you (or would you) like?

Walking/running_____

Biking_____

Swimming_____

Dancing_____

Competitive sports_____

Group exercise/aerobics class_____

Other_____

HOW do you like to be active?

Alone_____

With one friend_____

With a group_____

Now is the best time to be realistic in each of these areas! If you hate getting up early and don't like being cold, deciding to start a walking program at 6:00 a.m. in the winter will be the first step toward failure. Or, if you hate to work out alone and have purchased a workout video, but have not invited a friend to join you, realize your efforts will be frustrated from the start!

An active lifestyle should enhance the quality of your life, not add stress to it. If you do an activity you enjoy at the right time of day and in a comfortable environment, you will be setting yourself up for consistency and success.

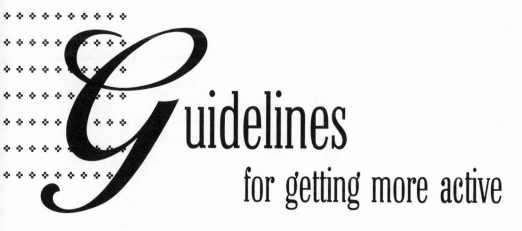

Guidelines
for getting more active

Positive Thought

There is a time when we must firmly choose the course we will follow, or the relentless drift of events will make the decision.

Herbert V. Prochnow

Practical Tip

As you are getting in touch with your physical self and learning to move around more in your environment, you'll find that your energy level will increase. But to be truly energized, you must enjoy the activity you are doing.

Today is a good day to start doing something... *anything*! After you are finished with today's reading, put down this book and get up and move.

Walking is a great way to increase your activity. Walking in pleasant places, especially with a friend or family member, is enjoyable for everyone. Take a walk around your neighborhood, a hike on the beach, or a stroll through a city park. If the weather won't permit outdoor activity, go to a shopping mall and walk briskly as you window-shop and people watch.

You may be able to walk only for a short distance right now, but stick with it and you'll find that your endurance will increase steadily. As you get into the habit of walking, try to walk whenever it fits into your day. A few short walks are just as beneficial from a health standpoint as one long session. If you can't find an hour to take a long walk right now, try to take three to four short walks. Active people report that a short burst of activity, like a walk around the block, can clear your head and re-energize you in the midst of the busiest day.

Guidelines for getting more active:

1. Consult a physician. Before starting any physical activity program, start with a physical examination by your doctor. Tell him or her that you plan to become more active and ask if there are any limits to the kinds of activities that you should do.

2. Listen to your body. Be aware of signs of strain or fatigue. You should be walking at a pace and distance that allows you to carry on a conversation. You should finish your exercise feeling energized, not exhausted.

3. Be patient. Your body will get stronger faster than you think. If you can only walk for five minutes right now, that five minutes is doing you a world of good. Keep it up!

4. Progress slowly, but steadily. The old saying "No pain, no gain" has led to a lot of injuries and discouragement. If you always work at a level that feels comfortable, or slightly harder than comfortable, you will progress slowly and steadily. Remember, we're looking at lifestyle changes and long-term gains, not just a quick fix.

Today's Accountability Check:

Did you walk today? ❑ Yes   ❑ No

How long?_____minutes

How do you feel?_____

Prayers & Passages

This is the day the LORD has made; let us rejoice and be glad in it.
Psalm 118:24

Patience, progress, and physical activity! I pray about them all the time. I guess, Lord, I must face the truth—I have only one day at a time to give, do, or be! Today, I will do something that I like to get me moving toward my goals. As always, Lord, I am asking you to help me—please! Amen.

Setting long-term goals

Positive Thought

Expenditure which begins at a great rate often comes to a sudden end by bankruptcy. Begin so that you can keep on, and even rise higher.

Charles Spurgeon

Practical Tip

A *goal* is "a mark on which to fix the eye." A goal should be a guiding, positive force that motivates and encourages you. It should give you focus and direction in each area of your life, and it should help you to evaluate or measure your efforts.

You will spend the next few days setting realistic goals. These goals will give you something tangible to look at when you need inspiration, and they will make you accountable when you want to chart your progress.

Long-term goals are those that you wish to achieve in the next five years. These goals allow you to dream. More important, long-term goals help you anticipate success and change in your life. Goals should set you up for success, not failure!

As you plan your long-term goals, make sure that they are realistic. They might seem unreachable now—and you may not know how you will achieve them—but if they are realistic, you will find a way. As your life moves forward, you can always come back if necessary and adjust your goals to keep them realistic.

Let's divide your long-term goals into four categories:

1. Physical: How do you see your physical self changing in five years? Exercising regularly, eating healthier, getting stronger and more fit, or taking up a new sport or activity might all be general long-term goals.

2. Mental: In the days ahead you may decide to read at least one book per month, visit an art museum, take a continuing education class, travel to a different country or state, change your job or vocation, or get an advanced degree.

3. Emotional: What would you like to change in your emotional makeup in the next five years? Maybe you want to get rid of your uncontrollable anger or a quick temper. Perhaps you are willing to admit to a chemical addiction or an eating disorder. Many of us struggle with memories that need healing and we have never consciously decided to work on them. Now may be the time to begin.

4. Spiritual: How would you like to grow in your spiritual life in the next five years? You might like to relinquish control of your life to God. Or perhaps you are ready for a closer walk with him. That goal might include praying and reading the Bible daily, memorizing Scripture, or teaching a Bible class. You may also decide to move into more active Christian service, volunteering as a camp counselor, a reading tutor, or a soup kitchen worker.

List at least three long-term goals in each of these areas:

Long-term physical goals:
1._____
2._____
3._____

Long-term emotional goals:
1._____
2._____
3._____

Long-term mental goals:
1._____
2._____
3._____

Long-term spiritual goals:
1._____
2._____
3._____

Prayers & Passages

Not that I have already obtained all this, or have already been made perfect, but I press on to take hold of that for which Christ Jesus took hold of me.

Philippians 3:12

Lord, I am so thankful that you go with me, have a plan for me, encourage me, and know all about my life! What would I do without Someone like you helping me make and move toward my goals? Thank you.

Setting short-term goals

Positive Thought

Victory is not won in miles but in inches. Win a little now, hold your ground, and later win a little more.

Louis L'Amour
(1908–1988)

Practical Tip

After setting long-term goals, the next step is to determine how you're going to achieve those goals. We've all fallen into the trap of wishing but never doing, or talking about our good intentions but never acting on them. Breaking down long-term goals into shorter goals will help you follow through on your wishes and good intentions. Short-term goals also allow you to chart your progress daily.

Take a moment to think about the goals you would like to achieve in one year. You will arrive at these one-year goals by taking each of your long-term goals and breaking them down into realistic short-term goals. For example, if you decided that one of your five-year goals is to exercise regularly, you now need to decide what you are going to do this year to make that happen. If you set a one-year goal to exercise at least three times each week, for at least thirty minutes each time, you will achieve that long-term goal in short-term steps.

Writing down your goals will keep you account-able and can act as a reminder and motivator when you start to lose momentum. The lists you create are to get you started, but you can take goal setting as far as you like. If you have more than three goals in an area of your life, write them all down.

Take each of your five-year goals and set a one-year goal that will move you toward achieving it:

Long-term goal (five years)
Short-term goal (one year)

Physical

_____   _____
_____   _____
_____   _____

Mental

_____   _____
_____   _____
_____   _____

Emotional

_____   _____
_____   _____
_____   _____

Spiritual

_____   _____
_____   _____
_____   _____

Today's Date:_____

Prayers & Passages

Have I not commanded you? Be strong and courageous. Do not be terrified; do not be discouraged, for the LORD your God will be with you wherever you go.
Joshua 1:9

Lord, I desire not only to *set* these goals for a lifestyle change, but to *achieve* them. Somehow I am not so afraid, knowing that you are with me. Give me an extra amount of courage for the days ahead, reminding me that each day is a new day and a fresh start. Here we go, Lord …

Setting 90-day goals

Positive Thought

When everybody tells you that you are being idealistic or impractical, consider the possibility that everybody could be wrong about what is right for you. Look inside yourself the way nobody else can. Will the pursuit of your dream hurt anybody? Do you stand at least a fair chance of success? If you fail, will you be seriously damaged or merely embarrassed? If you succeed, will it change your life for the better? When you can persuade yourself that your dream is worthwhile and achievable—then say thank you to the doubters and take the plunge…. How much better to know that we have dared to live our dreams than to live our lives in a lethargy of regret.

Gilbert E. Kaplan

Practical Tip

After setting your five-year and one-year goals, you are probably feeling quite motivated—maybe even excited—about making certain changes in your life. The next step is to become even more specific with your goals by making 90-day goals. You will find that returning to your list of goals frequently will provide you with inspiration as well as direction. These goals will be especially helpful when in the midst of your busy daily life you find yourself caught up in pursuing the urgent, rather than the important. At that point, go back to your goal list and get back on track.

It is essential that you consider time invested into your own physical, mental, emotional, and spiritual growth as valuable and important. Don't view it as selfish. Instead, look at it as putting fuel back into your tank, giving you the energy to give, share, and contribute effectively to the many areas in your life that demand your time.

Just think—soon your 90-day goals will be achieved and you will be able to acknowledge your success of setting and following through with a goal! To set 90-day goals, go back to your one-year goals and determine what you can do in the next 90 days to achieve them. Let's use our previous example of exercising regularly as a five-year goal, broken down into exercising three times a week for thirty minutes as a one-year goal. At this juncture, it would be easy to procrastinate and avoid exercising if you haven't decided exactly what you are going to do in those three weekly sessions. So, your 90-day goal might be to walk for thirty minutes on two of the days, and attend an aerobics class at a local YMCA on the third day. With a specific goal decided upon and written down, it will become harder for you to procrastinate or find excuses not to succeed.

List each of your one-year goals and set a specific 90-day goal that will help you achieve it.

	One-Year Goal	90-Day Goal
Physical	_____	_____
	_____	_____
	_____	_____
Mental	_____	_____
	_____	_____
	_____	_____
Emotional	_____	_____
	_____	_____
	_____	_____
Spiritual	_____	_____
	_____	_____
	_____	_____

Prayers & Passages

Being confident of this, that he who began a good work in you will carry it on to completion until the day of Christ Jesus.

Philippians 1:6

Lord, I am amazed that I can still hope and dream about goal setting, when I have struggled with goals before. But I am trusting that with your help and by writing down my plans, I can achieve these manageable and realistic goals. Oh, and Lord, if they're not realistic, please help me to recognize that and make any necessary adjustments even now. Amen.

 Setting daily goals

Positive Thought

A dream is what you would like for life to be and hold, but a goal is what you intend to make happen.

Dennis Waitley

Practical Tip

Daily goal setting will help you put your plan into your schedule. One of our favorite aspects of setting daily goals is that you can acknowledge your successes *every day!* When you set a goal for yourself and complete it, you get a double bonus. First, you feel great because you did something positive for yourself, and second, you feel great because you actually completed the goal that you set for yourself!

For daily goal setting, you'll return to your 90-day goals and determine where they can fit into your schedule each day. This step is very important. As we've all experienced, it is easy to get too busy, and only when it is too late, realize that because you didn't prioritize your goals, you didn't achieve them.

Using our ongoing example, once you've decided what kind of exercise you're going to do three times a week, you now need to decide when it fits into your schedule. For example, you might decide to walk early on Monday and Friday mornings and attend an aerobics class on Wednesday evening. When you prioritize your goals and actually place them into your schedule, you have the best chance of achieving them.

As you work on the following chart, use a pencil so that you can move your ideas around until all your goals have found a time slot. In addition, pull out your calendar and note any regular, on-going meetings or commitments that will affect your scheduling. This extra bit of planning from the start will increase your success-ability!

Now is the time to decide where each of your 90-day goals will fit into your schedule. Be specific about time and place. Then go for it!

	Physical Goals	Mental Goals	Emotional Goals	Spiritual Goals
MON.				
TUE.				
WED.				
THUR.				
FRI.				
SAT.				
SUN.				

Prayers & Passages

Let the morning bring me word of your unfailing love, for I have put my trust in you. Show me the way I should go, for to you I lift up my soul. Teach me to do your will, for you are my God; may your good Spirit lead me on level ground.
Psalm 143:8, 10

Write out a prayer that expresses your feelings, hopes, and fears—and ask God to be your guide.

_____

_____

_____

_____

_____

_____

_____

_____

_____

_____

_____

_____

_____

_____

Self-acceptance

✦✦
✦✦
✦✦

During this week, our focus will be on liking and accepting the person you are. Self-acceptance is elusive for many people. Therefore, this week we will focus on accepting yourself as you are today, while diligently pursuing the goals and changes you'd like to achieve in the future.

Week Two will help you balance your strengths and struggles and encourage you to discover what is really important to you. You will finish the week by writing your own personal mission statement, which will clearly define your values and beliefs.

Who am I?

Positive Thought

Where do you want to go in life? How do you want to get there? Do the roles you fill contribute to your goal? What do you do that is really important? What merely fills up time? In determining your best roles, keep those that advance you toward your goal and eliminate those that are useless and a drag. Your trouble may be too many good roles. You cannot afford to take on more than you can handle well.

Dr. Henry R. Brandt

Practical Tip

To accept yourself, you must first be aware of who you are, and then you must decide to like and accept that person. Even though we all have things that we'd like to change about ourselves, it's important that you accept who you are… *today.*

To help you define yourself, take a personal survey and answer the following question:

What are the five most important things in my life?

1._____
2._____
3._____
4._____
5._____

You probably listed things like: God, husband and children, career, home, parents, health, happiness, friends, church, community, world peace, etc. If you listed them randomly, go back through the list and number them in order of importance.

Using each item in your personal survey, make positive statements about who you are and what is important to you. Examples might be:

- ❖ I'm a devoted wife and mother who is trying to create a loving home for my family.
- ❖ I'm a struggling athlete who is working on getting fit and healthier.
- ❖ I'm active in my church and community and thankful that I have time and energy to give.

I'm_____

_____

I'm_____

_____

I'm_____

_____

I'm_____

_____

I'm_____

_____

Prayers & Passages

This is what the LORD says—your Redeemer, the Holy One of Israel: "I am the LORD your God, who teaches you what is best for you, who directs you in the way you should go."

Isaiah 48:17

Lord, I am often overwhelmed, overcommitted, and frustrated with the many roles and responsibilities in my daily life. Put me back on course, Lord. Though I feel as if I should go back to start over, I know that I can't feasibly do that. So I ask you to direct my steps forward today. Guide my heart. Help me to slow down. Grant me an extra measure of your Holy Spirit. Give me a deep desire for your order in my life. Amen.

Do I like myself?

Positive Thought

Personal soundness is not an absence of problems but a way of reacting to them.
Donald W. MacKinnon

Practical Tip

What do you like about yourself? Sometimes we find ourselves complaining about all of the things that we don't like about ourselves and would like to change, but we forget about all of the positive aspects of our personality and physical self.

What do you think are the positive aspects of yourself and your life? Some examples might be:

- ❖ I am an optimist and usually look at the bright side of things.
- ❖ I'm organized and get things done.
- ❖ I've cut a lot of junk food out of my diet.
- ❖ I teach my children about God throughout the day.

List at least six positive aspects that relate to your physical, mental, emotional, and spiritual self:

1._____

_____

2._____

_____

3._____

_____

4._____

_____

5._____

_____

6._____

_____

Now, write down just one aspect in each area of your life that you think needs changing. These may already be in your goals from last week. Be realistic about things that you don't like. Are they things that really need changing? Or are they things that you need to work at accepting? Some examples might be:

+ I get impatient with others who aren't as organized as I am.
+ I need to lose some weight and develop strength.
+ I wish I could find time for prayer each day.

1. Physical_____

_____

2. Mental_____

_____

3. Emotional_____

_____

4. Spiritual_____

_____

O LORD, you have searched me and you know me. You know when I sit and when I rise; you perceive my thoughts from afar. You discern my going out and my lying down; you are familiar with all my ways. Before a word is on my tongue you know it completely, O LORD. You hem me in—behind and before; you have laid your hand upon me.

Psalm 139:1–5

Write out your own prayer, reflecting on this passage:_____

_____

_____

_____

_____

_____

_____

_____

_____

_____

_____

_____

_____

Mirror, mirror...

Positive Thought

God grant me the serenity to accept the things I cannot change, courage to change the things I can, and the wisdom to know the difference.

The Serenity Prayer, attributed to Reinhold Niebuhr

Practical Tip

Do you ever find yourself standing in front of the mirror and thinking, "I wish I were thinner" or "I wish my nose wasn't so big"? Self-image plays a big part in every area of our life. A strong self-image can help you to become a happy and productive person, but a poor self-image can hold you back from great achievements.

What do you see when you look in the mirror? Describe yourself: _____ _____ _____ _____ _____

What would you like to see when you look in the mirror? Describe your ideal self: _____ _____ _____ _____ _____

Is this a realistic self-image? ❏ Yes ❏ No

If your ideal image isn't realistic or attainable, take some time to rethink your description of your ideal self. When you listed the five most important things in your life, your physical appearance probably wasn't one of them. Yet, for many people, concern about physical appearance takes precedence over concern about simple physical health.

The fact is, our body type and shape are—to a large extent—genetically pre-programmed. Our focus in *Thoroughly Fit* is to help you accept and celebrate the person that you are, while making lifestyle changes that will improve your quality of life. As you become more physically, mentally, emotionally, and spiritually fit, you may also be pleased to see changes in your appearance!

Now, take a minute and describe your <u>realistic</u> ideal self: _____
_____
_____
_____
_____
_____

Keep a picture of this healthy self in your head as you strive for balance in your life.

The value of values

Positive Thought

A person of integrity is one who has established a system of values against which all of life is judged.

V. Gilbert Beers of
Christianity Today

Practical Tip

As you pursue a balanced lifestyle, you can evaluate whether your current, actual behaviors match the values that you listed on Day 1 of this week. Ask yourself pointed questions: "How do I spend my time and energy? What kind of a pace do I keep?"

Use the chart on the next page to help you evaluate how balanced your life really is in relationship to your values. Once again, list your values ("The five most important things in your life" from Day 1), and across from each of those, list what you are doing right now to make that value a priority in your life. For example, if you listed good health as one of your values, ask: "Am I exercising regularly, eating moderately and healthfully, and getting enough rest?" If you listed spirituality as an important value, ask, "Am I spending time in a relationship with God, or do I go through rituals that mean nothing to me?"

When our time expenditure is equal to the values we hold dear, we can rejoice. But we will only reach that point if we are honest with ourselves about how we are spending our time. It is one thing to say that something is important to us. But if we never spend time nurturing or improving that area, that's an immediate red flag, waving to get our attention!

As you look at your chart, evaluate whether you are spending time on those things that you value the most.

Values	Amount of time	Do I need to re-prioritize my daily behavior? How?
1. _____	_____	_____
2. _____	_____	_____
3. _____	_____	_____
4. _____	_____	_____
5. _____	_____	_____

If you find that your daily behavior is in sharp contrast to what is important to you, begin today to prioritize the areas of your life that matter the most to you.

Prayers & Passages

Search me, O God, and know my heart; test me and know my anxious thoughts. See if there is any offensive way in me, and lead me in the way everlasting.

Psalm 139:23–24

Rewrite these verses in your own words. Then talk to God about the anxieties, concerns, and struggles you are facing at this time. Make this your personal prayer.

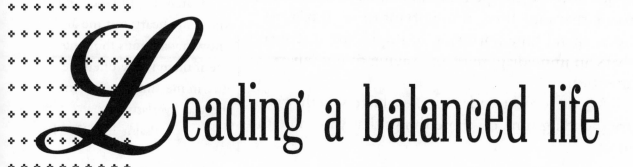

Leading a balanced life

Positive Thought

Convictions are the mainsprings of action, the driving powers of life. What a man lives are his convictions.

Francis C. Kelley

Practical Tip

You will achieve balance in your life if you evaluate yourself daily. Ask yourself, "Why am I doing all the things that I'm doing today? What do they mean in the whole scheme of life?"

In our culture, it's popular to be busy, to pursue a frantic lifestyle where every minute is filled with commitments. But this lifestyle may not be congruent with your values and goals. In fact, you may find yourself overwhelmed in certain areas, while neglecting other areas of your life. The result of the Week 2 surveys may show you that in order to achieve balance, you need to devote equal time and energy to the physical, emotional, mental, and spiritual areas of your life.

Use the chart on the next page to determine which areas of your life are in balance and which areas may be out of balance or need improvement. Put a check under the heading that most accurately reflects how you are doing in each area of your life.

Balanced Life Areas	Struggling	OK	Improving	Strong
Spiritual Life	❏	❏	❏	❏
Fitness/Activity	❏	❏	❏	❏
Healthful Eating/Nutrition	❏	❏	❏	❏
Mental/Professional Growth	❏	❏	❏	❏
Personal Time	❏	❏	❏	❏
Family Time	❏	❏	❏	❏
Social Relationships	❏	❏	❏	❏
Church Activities	❏	❏	❏	❏
Community Activities	❏	❏	❏	❏

In the next week, try to prioritize those areas in which you are struggling.

Prayers & Passages

Do not conform any longer to the pattern of this world, but be transformed by the renewing of your mind. Then you will be able to test and approve what God's will is—his good, pleasing and perfect will.

Romans 12:2

Lord, reflecting on my priorities and values has been a real eye-opener! I'm glad that you're on my side, that you are here to help me. I don't want to conform to my culture's pattern—that busyness equals success. Renew my mind, O Lord. Give me the courage to lead a balanced life. Amen.

Compare? Compete?

Consider this...

Positive Thought

Make enthusiasm your daily habit.

Don't let negative people determine your self-worth.

Get into the habit of talking to yourself affirmatively.

Get into the habit of using an affirmative, positive vocabulary.

Don't be a grudge collector.

Think positive and pleasing thoughts.

Don't brag.

Get high on doing good.

Don't give in to the ads and fads.

Wake up happy.

Find a positive support group.

Above all, make every day and every evening the best possible.

Dennis Waitley from
Being the Best

Practical Tip

You have just joined a health club and have resolved to exercise three times a week. But in your first aerobics class you have a hard time following the leader and learning the steps. Your moves are out of sync, and you can barely keep up with the pace. Meanwhile, little Miss Skinny is bouncing along in front of you, young, fit, tan, and beautiful. You decide that you'll never make it. You'll never learn the steps. You'll never get fit enough to keep up the pace. So you quit. And all your good intentions go down the drain.

As you try to lead a balanced lifestyle, don't fall into the trap of comparing yourself to someone else, or competing to be better than someone else. Unhealthy competition, uncontrolled jealousy, and habitual comparisons will only drain you of your joy, endurance, enthusiasm, and momentum.

When we are competitive, we crave to be better than someone else, and we forget that our focus should be on doing our best. When we compare ourselves to others, we forget that God made each of us unique, with our own strengths, weaknesses, and foibles. Competition does not bring us satisfaction—even when we're ahead. Nor does comparison. Instead, our satisfaction should rest on knowing that God has created us for a special purpose, and he asks only that we do our best for him.

For a unique twist on overcoming jealousy, try thinking of the other person as better than yourself. Sound odd? It's a biblical principle that has the power to release jealousy's control over you. In fact, once you have made a conscious decision to eliminate self-destructive thoughts, your relationships will relax, your personality will lighten up, and you will be free to move forward, knowing that you were made unique for your own special purpose. No one can do what you were perfectly created to do!

Think about three people of whom you are jealous or with whom you compete. List their names here and why you are jealous of them:

Name   Reason for jealousy
1._____   _____
2._____   _____
3._____   _____

Now, think of them as better than yourself. Then thank God for how he has created you, as a special person with your own gifts and talents.

Do nothing out of selfish ambition or vain conceit, but in humility consider others better than yourselves.

Philippians 2:3

Lord, I have to confess that I struggle even now with jealousy toward certain people. I confess that this creates tension between you and me, and between me and others. I'd like to move away from the negative thoughts and behaviors that trap me into comparing and competing. When I get those jealous feelings and thoughts, I'm going to recognize them as destructive and take the steps necessary to eliminate their power over me. This is a tough one, Lord. Help me! Amen.

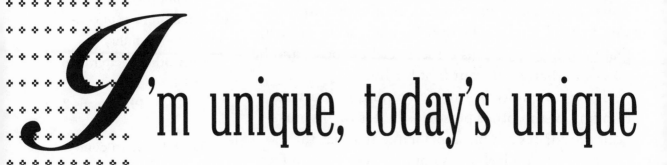

I'm unique, today's unique

Positive Thought

Our self-image strongly held essentially determines what we become.

Maxwell Maltz
(1899–1975)

Practical Tip

You've devoted time this week to discovering who you are and what really matters to you. Now you are ready to finish this week by writing your own personal mission statement.

Often companies or organizations will develop a mission statement that defines their values and beliefs. The day-to-day business decisions and activities of that company or organization revolve around that mission statement. Your mission statement will be a visual reminder of (1) what is important to you and (2) how you want to spend your time.

What is your "mission"? Today, take the time and thought necessary to create your mission statement by reviewing:

- ❖ your values,
- ❖ what you believe in, and
- ❖ the quality of life you want to live.

Write one or two sentences that summarize these thoughts._____

_____

_____

An example of your mission statement might be: "I will live each day with God as my guide, with love and respect for my family and friends, and with compassion for those who are in need. I will make time for myself to grow mentally and spiritually, and I will strive for a healthy lifestyle for myself and my family."

Before working on your mission statement, take just a few minutes to meditate quietly, think, and pray. Then try a few rough drafts—changing and rewording your thoughts until you hear yourself say, "That's it!" Finally, enter your mission statement below. You might want to recopy it onto an index card, post it where you will see it often, and share it with a few special people. Take the time to commit your mission statement to memory and remind yourself of it each day.

My Personal Mission Statement: _____
_____
_____
_____
_____
_____
_____
_____
_____
_____
_____
_____
_____
_____
_____
_____
_____
_____

Prayers & Passages

Trust in the LORD with all your heart and lean not on your own understanding; in all your ways acknowledge him, and he will make your paths straight.

Proverbs 3:5–6

It is incredible to consider that you have a plan for my life, Lord. I will trust you to walk with me through the paths that will lead me to fulfill my mission in life. Amen.

Self-care

❖ ❖
❖ ❖
❖ ❖

This is the week to learn to take care of yourself. You will start on an activity program, modify your eating behavior, and learn to schedule time for yourself. This week will give you guidelines for personalizing a program that fits your lifestyle.

You can do it!

Let's get moving

Positive Thought

No matter how far you have gone on a wrong road, turn back.

Turkish proverb

Practical Tip

Regardless of your previous lifestyle, research shows that increasing your activity level can help improve the quality of your life. Moderate, regular activity or exercise can give you the following physical and mental benefits:

- Maintain or improve your health,
- Reduce stress levels,
- Give you added energy, and
- Increase your longevity by decreasing the risk of heart disease.

The best news is that it's never too late to start! You can improve your condition at any age. If you find yourself making excuses such as "I don't have enough time" or "It doesn't fit into my day to exercise," check out this bit of information: Studies have found that people who increased their activity by doing just three ten-minute intervals of exercise a day showed significant increases in both fitness and health.

This finding means that you do not have to

spend hours every week at a gym to feel (and look!) a lot better; you can be more creative and resourceful, using brief ten-minute segments of exercise to increase your fitness.

Look at the following chart to see how you can increase your activity level. Then calculate the approximate number of calories you would be burning with simple activities.

Activity	Calories burned per 10 minutes
Gardening	40
Light Housework	30
Strolling (easy pace)	35
Walking moderately	50
Swimming (slowly)	50
Bicycling (moderately)	110
Square dancing	60
Aerobic dancing	60
Shopping	30
Tennis	65
Climbing stairs	70

Think about how you can include more activities into your day. Remember, if you can incorporate three ten-minute activity sessions, you will have accumulated thirty minutes of exercise in a day ... and you will reap all of the benefits!

Whatever you do, work at it with all your heart, as working for the Lord, not for men.

Colossians 3:23

Lord, help me to "make a move," to get up, get going, and get active. This may be easier than I have been willing to admit, and I may need a change of attitude about exercising. Please help me, Lord, because I can't do this alone. Thank you. Amen.

Taking the first step

Positive Thought

First do it, then say it.
Russian proverb quoted
by Sergei Bubka,
Russian pole-vaulter

Practical Tip ❖ ❖ ❖ ❖ ❖ ❖ ❖ ❖ ❖ ❖ ❖ ❖ ❖ ❖ ❖ ❖ ❖ ❖

Almost immediately, you will start to feel the benefits of increased activity! You may not see any changes in your physical shape for a few weeks, but you will begin to feel stronger right away. In addition, you will feel the emotional benefits of exercise after only the first session or two. You will have increased feelings of well-being, improved self-esteem, and a sense of accomplishment from setting and completing your goal of increased activity.

There are a number of shortcuts that you can take to integrate physical activity into your day. A few are listed below:

1. Walk up stairs, instead of taking an elevator or escalator.
2. Take a ten-minute walk at lunch or on your break at work.
3. Park farther from the entrance to the market, movies, or mall.
4. Play actively with your children at the park or at home.

5. Walk your dog ... or borrow a neighbor's!
6. Go window-shopping at a mall.
7. Make "activity dates" rather than lunch dates with friends. A walk is a great time to chat and catch up with each other.
8. Do housework vigorously and enjoy the double benefits you are reaping.
9. Do your own gardening or yard work.
10. Move around (instead of sitting) while you are talking on the phone.

Make a list of ways you can incorporate ten-minute activity sessions into your day:

Activity	When to fit it in
_____	_____
_____	_____
_____	_____
_____	_____
_____	_____
_____	_____
_____	_____
_____	_____
_____	_____
_____	_____
_____	_____
_____	_____

Prayers & Passages

God delights in each good step we take.

Psalm 37:23 (NKJV)

Lord, help me to take the steps that I know I must in order to become more active. Please open doors of opportunity for me. Nudge me to take advantage of them and strengthen me with each new day. Amen.

Cholesterol:
the good and the bad

Positive Thought

People should eat as they do in the Mediterranean on one day and as they do in the Orient on the next.

Scott Grundy,
University of Texas
Center of Human
Nutrition

Practical Tip

The word *cholesterol* is familiar to everyone. We see it on food labels, in advertising, and in newspaper headlines. But even though we talk about cholesterol, we often don't understand what it is and how it relates to our health and well-being.

Cholesterol is a waxy, fatlike substance that is in your bloodstream and in all the tissues in your body. It is found in all animals, and thus in all animal products we eat (meat, poultry, fish, eggs, and dairy products). Plant foods do not contain cholesterol. Most of the cholesterol in your blood is manufactured by your body, primarily by the liver. In addition, the average American consumes 400–500 milligrams of cholesterol in food each day. The cholesterol made by the body, and the cholesterol we eat in food both end up in the blood. *Some* cholesterol is necessary for vital body functions. But *excess* cholesterol is dangerous to the heart.

Excess cholesterol may accumulate in the walls of the blood vessels. This condition, called atherosclerosis, may ultimately cut off the flow of blood to the heart or brain and result in a heart attack or stroke. Since the body makes all the cholesterol it needs, you don't need to consume additional cholesterol to stay healthy.

Your total cholesterol is made up of three components. You may have heard about the "good cholesterol," which actually protects you against heart attacks. It's called HDL (high-density lipoprotein). The "bad cholesterol," which can increase your risk for heart disease, is called LDL (low-density lipoprotein). Triglycerides (fats) are the third component. LDL carries cholesterol through your system and leaves unused residues of cholesterol in your arterial walls. HDL circulates in the bloodstream, picking up cholesterol and bringing it back to the liver for reprocessing or excretion.

Most doctors look at your ratio of total cholesterol. This is found by dividing your total cholesterol by HDL .

If your ratio is above 4.5, you may be at a high risk for heart disease. A simple blood test by your doctor will give you these numbers. For example, if your total cholesterol is 240 and your HDL is 60, your cholesterol ratio is 4.0. This indicates a below-average risk for heart disease.

The factors that lower your total cholesterol are:
- Moderate exercise and weight reduction
- Low-fat eating habits (which will decrease cholesterol and LDL production)
- Low consumption of sugar and alcohol (which will increase triglycerides)

If you haven't started to eat more healthfully and become more active already, this may be the factor you need to get motivated!

The power of a partner

Positive Thought

Two are better than one, because they have a good return for their work: If one falls down, his friend can help him up. But pity the man who falls and has no one to help him up!

Ecclesiastes 4:9–10

Practical Tip

Staying motivated to make lifestyle changes can be difficult if you try to do it alone. When you recruit family or friends to join you it is a lot easier to become and stay motivated. A partner—or partners—will also keep you accountable, and can gently but firmly remind you when you are slipping.

Look at the areas of your life in which you've decided to make changes. In each area is there a person or persons that you can team up with to share the goals and rewards? You might find a friend to take a walk with each day; you will find that keeping an appointment with her makes it difficult to procrastinate and avoid that activity. Maybe your spouse or roommate can be your partner in more healthful eating. Planning and sharing good meals together will motivate both of you to stick to your plan. Tell your family that you are trying to take thirty minutes a day for your own mental or spiritual growth and that you need their help to give you that time. Or you might ask a friend to memorize a Scripture verse each month with you.

Below, list one change or goal you are trying to achieve in each of the four lifestyle areas. Then write down the name of someone who might be a good partner to help you stay committed. Finally, complete the rest of the questions.

Physical:_____

Partner:_____

Phone number:_____

When you will call them:_____

What you will ask them:_____

Did they respond?_____

What is the plan?_____

Mental:_____

Partner:_____

Phone number:_____

When you will call them:_____

What you will ask them:_____

Did they respond?_____

What is the plan?_____

Emotional:_____

Partner:_____

Phone number:_____

When you will call them:_____

What you will ask them:_____

Did they respond?_____

What is the plan?_____

Spiritual:_____

Partner:_____

Phone number:_____

When you will call them:_____

What you will ask them:_____

Did they respond?_____

What is the plan?_____

Prayers & Passages

"Again, I tell you that if two of you on earth agree about anything you ask for, it will be done for you by my Father in heaven. For where two or three come together in my name, there am I with them."

Matthew 18:19–20

Lord, you did send many out in twos—Moses and Aaron, Caleb and Joshua, Naomi and Ruth—please provide for me some power-partners for my 90-day journey. I confess that I want to be accountable, Lord, and that I need help. Please send a friend. Amen.

Make an appointment

Positive Thought

Don't pray just when you feel like it. Make an appointment with the King and keep it.

Corrie ten Boom

Practical Tip

I have found that making and keeping an appointment equals accountability—in *any* area!

Wouldn't you agree that a meeting, workout class, appointment, or engagement that you consider important is usually placed on your calendar? And why? So that ...

- ❖ you don't forget it,
- ❖ you plan around and for it,
- ❖ you don't double book, and
- ❖ you *keep* it!

There came a point in my life—at age twenty-eight—when I [Becky] had to admit that I had gotten so busy *doing* good (and urgent) things that I had lost the balance in my own life. I realized that every single day I was too busy! It was then that I had to stop everything and re-evaluate.

Though I am not a very serious or quiet person, I am a spiritual person. After much soul-searching, I came to the conclusion that spending one hour each day in a quiet time, reading God's Word and talking with him by journaling, was the best way for me to balance every area of my life.

And even though I always believed that prayer and quiet time were good things, I did not succeed with my quiet time until I made it a priority by putting my "Appointment with the King" on my daily calendar. For ten years now, for one hour every day, I read the Bible, listen, reflect, pray, confess, and quiet my busy self. I am convinced that this practice has improved every area of my life by keeping me accountable, developing my character, directing my future, and making me more productive and focused.

1. Have you ever had an appointment with God? Describe:_____
_____
_____

2. Have you ever tried writing your thoughts and prayers to God? Explain._____
_____
_____

3. If you were to spend time with God every day, what part of your day would be good for a quiet time of reflection and prayer? (for example, before breakfast, children's naptime, before going to bed)
_____
_____
_____

4. What amount of time would be comfortable for you to spend with God? _____
_____
_____

5. Give it a try—put your appointment with the King on the calendar!_____
_____
_____

Prayers & Passages

Show me your ways, O LORD, teach me your paths; guide me in your truth and teach me, for you are God my Savior, and my hope is in you all day long.

Psalm 25:4–5

Try writing (or journaling) a prayer to God. Talk to him as you would a dear friend whom you love and respect._____
_____
_____
_____
_____
_____
_____
_____
_____
_____
_____
_____
_____
_____
_____
_____
_____
_____
_____
_____
_____
_____
_____

The balancing act

Positive Thought

Pace yourself. Live to see your success.

Dennis Waitley

Practical Tip ✦

Women, especially since the seventies, have been killing themselves with the super-woman image. Some women are working moms, climbing the corporate ladder during the day and caring for their families on evenings and weekends. Other mothers are busy at home with their children, running a home and juggling numerous responsibilities.

Our greatest asset is our individuality. We each have certain talents, energy levels, financial responsibilities, family obligations, and aspirations. All of those factors go into the equation for balancing our lives. As you think of ways to balance your life, consider some of these creative alternatives:

* Decrease hours worked and income earned in order to stay at home while children are young.
* Work ten hours a day for four days—then stay at home three days.
* Hire a house cleaner once a week (find a high-school or college student who is less expensive and needs extra cash).

- Work at home and hire part-time babysitters to help during non-nap times.
- Work out at 6:00 a.m. to home videos or cable channels before going to work.
- Find a friend to walk with during the lunch break at work.
- Schedule in a library visit one time a month.
- Go on a retreat with a spouse, friend, or by yourself to go over your calendar and your commitments.

Can you think of anyone you know who models a balanced life?_____
_____
_____

What areas might you need to re-evaluate in order to bring more balance into your life?_____
_____
_____

What is one change you could incorporate into your life today?_____
_____
_____

We can all probably list the names of people who have lost family because their jobs consumed them, or burned out in volunteer work because they never said "no," or found themselves without a social life because of making work and money their whole life, or have quit going to church in order to have more rest and relaxation. In making lifestyle changes, however, you are seeking a balance that will enhance your quality of life, improve your relationships, and develop a strong character.

"Do not store up for yourselves treasures on earth, where moth and rust destroy, and where thieves break in and steal. But store up for yourselves treasures in heaven, where moth and rust do not destroy, and where thieves do not break in and steal. For where your treasure is, there your heart will be also."

Matthew 6:19–21

Lord, help me to treasure people more than things … to know you better and your will for me … I love you.

A daily food guide

Positive Thought

Eat to live, and not live to eat.
Benjamin Franklin,
Poor Richard's Almanac

Practical Tip

We've already discussed lifestyle changes in your activity level. Now let's look at how to make lifestyle changes in the way you approach nutrition and eating.

Most people do not succeed with diets because food restriction is unpleasant and does not teach you how to modify your eating behavior for long-term changes. Your goal should not be to lose weight or to diet successfully. Instead, your goal should be to learn how to make healthy, low-fat food choices. Food, just like exercise, should be approached with the principles of balance, variety, and moderation. Eating should give us energy—as well as pleasure!

An easy way to make sure you are eating a balanced diet from all the food groups is to use the USDA's new Food Guide Pyramid. The Pyramid shows you which foods fall into each food group and tells you how much of each food you should eat each day for healthful nutrition. As you can see from the chart, grains (bread, cereal, rice, and pasta) form the base of the pyramid, meaning you need to eat the most from this group. Fruits and vegetables form the next level, followed by proteins such as meat, fish, poultry, eggs and nuts, and dairy products such as milk, cheese, and yogurt. The small tip of the pyramid shows fats, oils, and sweets. Eat the recommended number of servings daily in each food group, and remember, you can choose the foods you like within that food group!

The pyramid tells you to eat six to eleven servings from the grain group and two to four servings from the fruit group. But how do you know how much is a serving? Use the following guide to determine what counts as a serving. A turkey sandwich, for example, would count as two servings of grains and one serving of poultry. Tomato and lettuce on it could add one to two servings of vegetables.

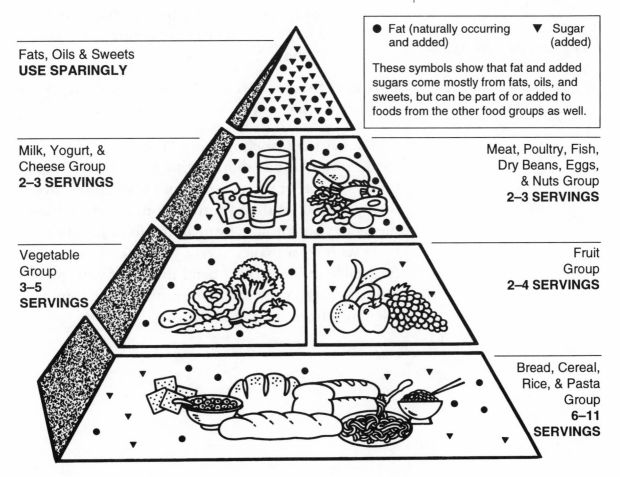

Fats, Oils & Sweets
USE SPARINGLY

● Fat (naturally occurring and added)　▼ Sugar (added)

These symbols show that fat and added sugars come mostly from fats, oils, and sweets, but can be part of or added to foods from the other food groups as well.

Milk, Yogurt, & Cheese Group
2–3 SERVINGS

Meat, Poultry, Fish, Dry Beans, Eggs, & Nuts Group
2–3 SERVINGS

Vegetable Group
3–5 SERVINGS

Fruit Group
2–4 SERVINGS

Bread, Cereal, Rice, & Pasta Group
6–11 SERVINGS

Prayers & Passages

For the eyes of the LORD range throughout the earth to strengthen those whose hearts are fully committed to him.

2 Chronicles 16:9

Lord, I'd like to make changes in the way that I eat and glorify you by respecting this body that you lovingly created. Help me to make gradual changes in my eating habits. Thank you for the nourishment that you provide my body, my mind, and my spirit. Amen.

How much is a serving? (Adult serving sizes)

Grain Group: 1 slice of bread; 1 ounce of cereal, 1/2 cup cooked rice, pasta, or cooked cereal

Vegetable Group: 1 cup raw leafy vegetables; 1/2 cup other vegetables (raw or cooked)

Fruit Group: 1 medium apple, banana, orange, or melon wedge; 3/4 cup juice; 1/2 cup canned or cooked fruit

Dairy Group: 1 cup milk or yogurt; 1 1/2 ounces of cheese

Meat Group: 2–3 ounces cooked lean meat, poultry, or fish; 1 egg, 2 tablespoons peanut butter, and 1/2 cup cooked beans all count as 1 ounce of meat (about 1/3 serving)

Fats and Sweets Group: Limit your calories from these to tiny amounts.

Rather than labeling foods "good" or "bad" foods, simply think about eating more foods from the lower half of the pyramid and fewer foods from the upper half of the pyramid. Consider the fat and sugars in your choices from all the food groups. Pasta with cream sauce (grain group) or french fries (vegetable group) will expand the tip of your pyramid and make your diet less healthful than lower fat selections from the same groups.

PART TWO

Motivation

Motivation is the basis for your actions and decisions and the key to achieving your goals. To help you get motivated and stay motivated, in the next three weeks we will look at: facing changes, facing choices, and facing challenges.

Facing Changes

❖ ❖
❖ ❖
❖ ❖

Let's face it—making lifestyle changes requires *change!* As you make lifestyle changes, we want to encourage you to notice, experience, and "feel the difference" in your body, mind, and soul. As we focus on change this week, we'll give you practical ways to change your eating and activity habits. Week 4 encourages you to make emotional changes during times of trial and transition.

This is the week to face change with a positive mental outlook—and allow it into your life.

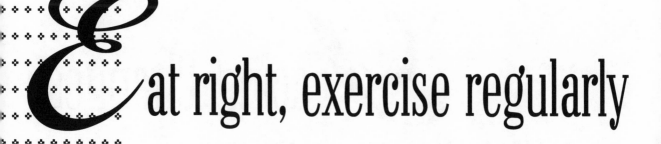

Eat right, exercise regularly

Positive Thought

The only way to change one's body weight is to begin a lifelong series of new habits.

Dr. Jules Hirsch

Practical Tip

Many people search for the quick health fix that will keep them strong and in good physical shape. But health can never be achieved through quick-fix methods. Rather, physical fitness is developed over time simply by exercising moderately and regularly and by developing moderate, healthy eating habits.

Perhaps you are surprised that we stress moderation in exercise and eating habits. After all, isn't exercising supposed to be strenuous and exhausting? Doesn't eating right mean that we have to deprive ourselves of all the foods we love, complain about our diets, and feel guilty when we blow them?

No! We have found that people are not motivated by guilt, nor will they eat food they don't enjoy, or do exercises that bore them. In the nineties, the health and fitness industry has revised their "no pain, no gain" philosophy and developed a new "kinder, gentler" approach to fitness—a moderate approach that can and will lead to success.

We want to encourage you to use words such as moderation and consistency when you discuss your exercise and eating habits. These will bring you to your goals faster and safer than a quick-fix method.

Moderation means finding the balance between extremes. Instead of strict diets or wild junk food binges, eat all foods in moderate quantities. As a moderately active individual, you will fall somewhere between a marathoner and a couch potato, but you will still enjoy great health.

Consistency, rather than intensity, is the answer to the question, "How can I get results?" As you make it a daily habit to prioritize your physical health, you will find that it becomes easier to make exercise and healthful eating an integral part of every day.

Look for and build into your daily routine opportunities for activity. Remember that a bit of activity here, a bit of activity there, will add up. The cumulative effects of small efforts over time reap rewards.

Ways to plan ahead for healthy eating on a daily basis could include keeping healthy snacks in your fridge. Or this might be a perfect time to treat yourself to a new, healthy, lowfat cookbook!

If you have a hard time staying consistent with the lifestyle changes that you are trying to make, think for a minute about all of the positive aspects that the changes will make. Develop a positive picture in your mind regarding eating and activity.

Below, list some positive benefits that would result from being active regularly and from eating healthily:

Regular Activity _____

Eating Healthy _____

The next mental step to take is to see yourself as the beneficiary of these results. Ask yourself, "How does it look on me? How do I feel? Would it be worth the effort?"

Enjoy your activities

Positive Thought

Be sure to keep busy, so the devil may always find you occupied.

Flavius Vegetius Renatus

Practical Tip

Scientists that study the relationship between health and exercise have concluded that there are health benefits to all types of activity. They conclude that it is not so much *what* activity you choose, but that you stay active!

A long-term Harvard University study of nearly 17,000 people showed that those who burned 2,000 "activity calories" per week had longer life spans than those sedentary people who burned fewer than 500 "activity calories" per week. "Activity calories" are those calories burned while engaging in movement—which can be either structured or unstructured to be effective.

Let's look at three ways to add "activity calories" to your daily schedule:

1. Formal activity: If you can make time for regularly scheduled exercise sessions such as walking, aerobics, swimming, cycling, or weight training, you will be burning "activity calories" and improving your fitness level. To improve your fitness and health, you should perform these activities at least three times per week, and for a minimum of twenty to thirty minutes each time. (Note: Of these three types of activities, formal activity takes the most motivation and determination to keep doing consistently.)

2. Functional activity: If you can't find time to schedule formal activity into your day, or you find it difficult to maintain the motivation necessary to stick with a formal program, functional activity may be just for you. If you can walk to work, bike to the store, take the stairs instead of the elevator, do your own gardening, or clean your house vigorously, you are burning "activity calories" while you fulfill your obligations and cope with your busy schedule.

3. Fun activity: What kind of recreational activities sound like fun to you? Your list might include rollerblading, going on a hike, or playing golf, volleyball, or tennis. A game of softball with your children or a bike ride with the family would also be fun ways to spend part of a weekend. The key is to find an activity that is enjoyable to you. You will be amazed how much easier it is to stick with your commitment to being active if you choose activities that are fun for you to do.

Ideally, some combination of the three categories of activity above will work for you. Take a moment to think about your week. Decide what type of activity fits most easily into each day and is enjoyable for you. Make a few notes._____

_____

_____

_____

Remember: You will stay more motivated if these activities fit conveniently and easily into your schedule.

Prayers & Passages

All hard work brings a profit, but mere talk leads only to poverty.
                    Proverbs 14:23

Lord, help me to enjoy being active! Help me to look honestly at my schedule and see how exercise and activity can fit—with ease—into my life. I need your guidance and discernment. Amen.

Don't hold back—
move ahead!

Positive Thought

The chief pang of most trials is not so much the actual suffering itself as our own spirit of resistance to it.

Jean Nicolas Grou

Practical Tip

Change is a frightening aspect of life for most of us. It is difficult to alter our lives, even if the changes are positive ones. There is some comfort in the fact that if we just keep going on as we have been, we don't have to take the risk of challenges, or invest time and energy, or deal with the unknown factors that will come up if we allow "change" to enter into our lives.

In order to face change positively, we should understand the process that allows change to take place. This process has four steps:

1. Decide that you want to make some changes in your life.

2. Identify the fears that may hold you back and cause inaction.

3. List the positive aspects associated with this change.

4. Commit to one or more measurable actions that will cause you to change and will help overcome your fears or reservations.

Going through this process will help you clarify

exactly why and how you are making changes.

Here is a sample. If you feel that you are weak in the spiritual area of your life, you must first decide that you want to grow in your relationship with God. Then you might list the fears that have held you back: (1) being afraid to give up control of your life to God, or (2) fearing your friends will think you are weak or crazy.

Next, list the positive aspects that change would bring to your spiritual growth: (1) a peace in knowing that God is in control, and (2) your friends might see the changes in your life and seek those changes for themselves.

Last, commit to actions that will take your desire to grow from thought to actuality: (1) spend 20 minutes each day reading, praying, and developing your relationship with God, and (2) regularly attend a church where you can worship, serve, and fellowship.

Now you try it ...

List one change that you have decided you'd like to make in your life, and go through this four-step process:

1. I would like to change _____ in my life.
2. Fears that hold me back from making this change are:_____

_____

3. Positive effects that this change can bring would be:_____

_____

4. Actions I plan to take to make this change happen:_____

_____

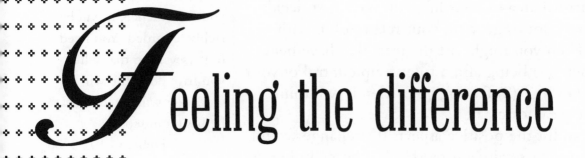

Feeling the difference

Positive Thought

Men and women who lack genuine self-esteem and rely on their physical attributes to feel good about themselves inevitably will do everything they can to preserve their looks—the external—but will do very little to develop their inner value and worth.

Dennis Waitley

Practical Tip

The mirror and the scale can be your friends—or your enemies—depending on how you perceive yourself. Your body image is the picture you have of your body, how it looks to you, and how you think it looks to others. People who are overly concerned about their body image continually pursue an external picture of themselves being thin and beautiful like the models and movie stars they see in magazines and on the screen.

Our society definitely focuses on the outward aspects of beauty, instead of focusing on having good health, a positive mental attitude, or a spiritual outlook on life. As you make lifestyle changes, we want to encourage you to notice, experience, and "feel the differences" in your emotional, spiritual, and physical health—rather than focusing only on outward results seen in a mirror.

Use the following checklist to examine how you feel about your body image:

	Never	Sometimes	Always
1. I am concerned about how I look.	❏	❏	❏
2. I think that I am overweight.	❏	❏	❏
3. I get on the scale and worry about my weight.	❏	❏	❏
4. I wish I were in better shape.	❏	❏	❏
5. I look at models and envy their looks.	❏	❏	❏
6. I don't believe my friends and family when they tell me I look fine.	❏	❏	❏

If you answered "always" more than three times, you may be more preoccupied with your body image than with your health. This week, and ultimately forever, try to take your focus off your external appearance and concentrate on how you feel each day. At the end of the day, if you have made an effort to balance each area of your life, congratulate yourself on your efforts and take a minute to *feel the difference!*

Prayers & Passages

Therefore, I urge you, brothers, in view of God's mercy, to offer your bodies as living sacrifices, holy and pleasing to God—this is your spiritual act of worship. Do not conform any longer to the pattern of this world, but be transformed by the renewing of your mind. Then you will be able to test and approve what God's will is—his good, pleasing and perfect will.

Romans 12:1–2

Lord, I've struggled so often with not liking how I look … with wanting to look like someone else, making myself miserable with discontent, and wasting a lot of time and thought on the "ultimate" outward appearance. Forgive me, Lord. I ask you to renew my mind and change my thoughts to be more like yours. Thank you. Amen.

Exchanges
(making healthy substitutions)

Positive Thought

Since habits become power, make them work with you and not against you.

E. Stanley Jones

Practical Tip ••••••••••••••••••••••••••••

As we focus on change this week, let's look at some practical changes that you can easily make in your eating habits. Exchanging high-fat and less nutritious foods for lower-fat, more nutritious foods will make a big difference in the quality of your meals. Just by implementing this simple change, you will decrease your fat intake, lower your cholesterol, and reduce your caloric intake. Whether you like quick-to-fix microwave cooking, or gourmet cuisine, you really can shop, cook, and eat healthier today by making certain exchanges.

We've listed a number of substitutions that you can make to enhance the quality of your eating:

Instead of this …
    Cream cheese on a bagel
    Sour cream on baked potato
    Ice cream sundae
    High-fat salad dressing
    Peanuts
    Cake with icing
    Potato chips and dip

Candy bar
Doughnut or pastry
Hamburger on a bun
Mayonnaise
Ice cream bar
Cheese on pasta

Try this …
Nonfat ricotta cheese on a bagel
Nonfat yogurt mixed with chives on potato
Nonfat frozen yogurt topped with fruit
Low- or non-fat bottled dressing
Pretzels
Angel food cake with fresh strawberries
Baked tortilla chips and salsa
Low-fat muffin or high-fiber pancakes
Low-fat granola bar or a piece of fruit (grapes)
Grilled chicken on whole wheat roll
Mustard
Frozen fruit bar
Nonfat cottage cheese on pasta

What exchanges can you begin to incorporate into your meals this week? _____
_____
_____
_____

As a reminder, post on the refrigerator a list of exchanges that you would be willing to make. Then follow them until they become habit!

Prayers & Passages

It is not good to eat too much honey, nor is it honorable to seek one's own honor. Like a city whose walls are broken down is a man who lacks self-control.
Proverbs 25:27–28

Lord, when I think of giving up something I like, I am either afraid—or stubborn. But when I think about exchanging foods that I like or could learn to like for foods that will always hinder me from reaching my goals, I feel ready. Lord, I acknowledge that I am finally willing to make the choices and exchanges that will help me on my journey in making lifestyle changes. Signed _____.

ransition time

Positive Thought

Never despair, but if you do, work on in despair.
Edmund Burke
(1729–1797)

Practical Tip ••••••••••••••••••••••••••

In the midst of balancing the physical, mental, emotional, and spiritual areas of your life, you may be interrupted by certain events that make it difficult to stick with the goals you have set for yourself. For example, you may move to a new city, change jobs, or have a child, and suddenly all that was old, comfortable, and easy has become new and uncertain. Or you may experience smaller changes, such as the start of school, a vacation, or relatives visiting your home.

Whatever the change, you will need a transition time to rethink your schedule and priorities. But you should recognize that during a transition it is still possible to make time for your physical, mental, emotional, and spiritual growth.

For example, if you are moving your family to a new city, you may need to forgo your "three times a week walk" for a few weeks, until you get settled. During this time, however, you can take advantage of functional activities and congratulate yourself for all the exercise you are getting as you lift, carry, and unpack boxes. And take advantage of fun activities also, like getting the whole family out for a walk around the block to explore your new neighborhood.

If you can't cook healthy meals during this period, don't despair. Choose pizza or pasta and a salad bar instead of fast-food burgers and fries. Try to carve out even ten minutes a day for yourself to read or pray. Remind yourself that your continued emotional and spiritual growth makes it easier to cope with the stresses that a transition can bring into your life.

If you find that your forward momentum has stopped altogether, it's never too late to start up again. Return to your goals and mission statement and review them, then be encouraged to move forward again.

Have you experienced any change or transition recently? If so, explain:_____
_____
_____
_____
_____
_____

What can you do to creatively include healthy eating and functional activity during this time? _____
_____
_____
_____
_____
_____

Wait for the LORD; be strong and take heart and wait for the LORD.
Psalm 27:14

Write your own prayer, sharing your feelings and frustrations. Then ask God to help you in specific ways.

Dear Lord ..._____
_____
_____
_____
_____
_____
_____
_____
_____
_____
_____
_____
_____
_____
_____
_____
_____
_____

Take a leap—of faith

Positive Thought

I have held many things in my hands, and I have lost them all; but whatever I have placed in God's hands, that I still possess.

Martin Luther

Practical Tip

In 1976, I [Becky] finally admitted to myself and others that I was an alcoholic. Even though I was only twenty-one years old, I had struggled for years with low self-esteem, a dysfunctional family, and the desire to be popular. And I was running from God. I lived on the edge, always looking for fun and adventure as a way to escape from my emotional pains and the negative situations I got involved with while drinking and on drugs.

The escapades finally ended when I simply admitted that my life was out of control. (This is step 1 in Alcoholics Anonymous Twelve Steps.)

Like the millions of alcoholics, drug addicts and over-eaters in America, I realized that I needed help from someone who was bigger than my problem (step 2).

Three weeks later, I asked God to help me, change me, forgive me, and give me a fresh start (step 3).

The repercussions of that prayer began from the inside out. I did change my lifestyle—and was forced to change my friends and my hangouts. I began to dress, talk, and act differently.

I look back over more than sixteen years of sobriety and realize that it all began with a giant leap of faith into God's arms. I'm just so glad that he waits for "prodigals" like me to come home!

Are you at a time where your life is out of control or unmanageable? Explain:_____
_____
_____
_____
_____
_____
_____
_____
_____
_____
_____
_____
_____

Therefore, if anyone is in Christ, he is a new creation; the old has gone, the new has come!
2 Corinthians 5:17

Perhaps you'd like to take a leap of faith today, to admit that your life is unmanageable and that you need help. Perhaps you'd like to acknowledge that God can help you. Then make this your prayer ...

_____
_____
_____
_____
_____
_____
_____
_____
_____
_____
_____
_____
_____
_____
_____
_____
_____

Facing Choices

✦ ✦

✦ ✦

✦ ✦

Do you enjoy going to a great new restaurant and reading the menu? Or flipping through a catalog to plan your Christmas shopping? Or dreaming about where your next vacation will be? Choices make life fun and interesting! Week 5 gives numerous ideas on how you can make healthy choices in the way you eat, think, and act. This week will remind you that the choices you've made toward a balanced lifestyle are important—important enough to make the time and take the time to achieve them. Go for it!

Cross-training

Positive Thought

Keep making the move-ments of life.
Thornton Wilder

Practical Tip

Cross-training is a popular term for a simple concept. It means changing from day to day or week to week the activities that you do. Cross-training has a number of benefits:

- Keeps you from getting bored with the same activity all the time.
- Uses different muscles with each activity, so that you will balance your muscle strength.
- Reduces the risk of injury associated with performing the same activity, exercise, or sport continually.
- Allows you to change activities with the season or time of day.
- Balances more active or challenging activities with less active, easier ones.

The idea behind cross-training is to mix and match your activities throughout the week. You can choose from formal activities, functional activities, and fun activities. Here is one example of using the cross-training method within a weeks' period:

Monday: thirty-minute brisk walk with a friend (formal)
Tuesday: played at the park with children/did housework (functional and fun)
Wednesday: walked to work/took the stairs to the fifth floor/walked home (functional)
Thursday: twenty-minute bike ride/played ball with children (formal and fun)
Friday: thirty-minute walk with a friend (formal)
Saturday: softball game at the park/gardening (fun and functional)
Sunday: walk on the beach with the family (fun)

Use the cross-training chart below to determine the types of exercises you can fit into your schedule this week:

	Formal	Functional	Fun
Monday:	_____	_____	_____
Tuesday:	_____	_____	_____
Wednesday	_____	_____	_____
Thursday:	_____	_____	_____
Friday:	_____	_____	_____
Saturday:	_____	_____	_____
Sunday:	_____	_____	_____

Prayers & Passages

So whether you eat or drink or whatever you do, do it all for the glory of God.

1 Corinthians 10:31

Thank you, Lord, that every day has within it an opportunity to be active. Thank you, Lord, that I am learning to make and take time to be active. Thank you, Lord, that ... (Write down some things for which you are thankful.)

_____
_____
_____
_____
_____
_____
_____
_____
_____
_____
_____
_____
_____
_____
_____
_____

Amen.

Pace yourself

Positive Thought

Each runner has a different finish line—the goal each person has set.

Dennis Waitley

Practical Tip

Pace yourself. If you set goals or tasks for yourself that progress too quickly, you might be setting yourself up for failure. It is very important to progress at a rate that is comfortable for you in each of the lifestyle areas in which you are seeking growth. Progress in each area of a balanced life should look something like this:

Physical: Progressing slowly and sensibly in the area of activity or exercise is important to help prevent injuries or sore muscles. The perceived exertion test is a good way to determine if you are working too hard in an activity. Simply ask yourself how you feel during the particular activity. If you can carry on a conversation, don't feel too out of breath, and finish the activity feeling as if you could do a little more, you are working and progressing at a pace that is right for you.

As you grow in your nutritional awareness, implement one dietary change at a time. If you make changes too quickly, you and your family may feel overwhelmed and deprived of the foods that you are used to eating. Instead, gradually substitute healthier foods, and they will eventually become a part of your lifestyle. You will forget that you ever ate any other way!

Mental: Progress to your mental goals may be quick and exciting as you complete each chapter of the book you chose to read, or slow and steady as you work toward the college degree you decided to pursue. If you find yourself getting frustrated with goals that will take a long time to complete, remember that it's okay to break those long-term goals down into shorter goals that are easier to attain. Congratulate yourself when you finish a book, expand your mind with lectures on audio tapes, or attend a class to learn new skills.

Emotional: Be patient with yourself as you work toward the emotional goals that you have set for yourself. You may see faster progress in the physical area of your life, but remind yourself that your pace and progress will vary in each area. If you are receiving counseling, attending a support group, or reading self-help books, if you are becoming aware of your failings and becoming willing to change them, you will progress steadily.

Spiritual: Progress in the spiritual area of your life is directly related to the time you invest in study of the Bible, in fellowship, in Christian service, and especially in prayer. Your pace in this area will be dictated by consistency. You will experience progress if you will spend time with God—even a small amount—each day.

In what area of your life are you most ready for progress? Explain: _____
_____
_____
_____

Prayers & Passages

Do you not know that in a race all the runners run, but only one gets the prize? Run in such a way as to get the prize. Everyone who competes in the games goes into strict training. They do it to get a crown that will not last; but we do it to get a crown that will last forever. Therefore I do not run like a man running aimlessly; I do not fight like a man beating the air. No, I beat my body and make it my slave so that after I have preached to others, I myself will not be disqualified for the prize.

1 Corinthians 9:24–27

Lord, I've never been very consistent or diligent … but I am very willing to try. I want to pace myself, to live a balanced life, to progress in every area of my life. Give me a deep desire to reach the goals I have set for this 90-day journey. Thank you.

 ecide not to give up

Positive Thought

Perseverance is a great element of success. If you only knock long enough and loud enough at the gate, you are sure to wake up somebody.

Henry Wadsworth Longfellow (1807–1882)

Practical Tip

One of your ongoing challenges in making a lifestyle change will be to persevere and not give up. As you look at your progress, pace, and patterns of growth in each lifestyle area, let's review yesterday's Practical Tip:

Physical: In improving yourself physically, there are many options to pursue, but remember, whenever trying any new activity or sport, go at a pace that feels easy until you get used to it. If you are progressing at the appropriate rate for your level of fitness, you shouldn't feel exhausted, sore, or discouraged.

Mental and Emotional: In these two areas, you will often need outside sources to stimulate your growth. Are you regularly reading books that stretch you mentally and emotionally? Do you attend a support or small group? Are you journaling?

Spiritual: Especially because the spiritual area involves a relationship, spending time with God will be the key to developing a more intimate relationship with him as your friend, confidant, counselor, Lord, and Savior.

Now take a moment to ask yourself a few questions about your pace:

	Stalled	Snail's pace	Walk	Jog	Run
1. What is my pace?					
Physical	❏	❏	❏	❏	❏
Mental	❏	❏	❏	❏	❏
Emotional	❏	❏	❏	❏	❏
Spiritual	❏	❏	❏	❏	❏

	None	Little	Some	Much	Tons
2. Do I feel progress?					
Physical	❏	❏	❏	❏	❏
Mental	❏	❏	❏	❏	❏
Emotional	❏	❏	❏	❏	❏
Spiritual	❏	❏	❏	❏	❏

	Get going!	Pick up the beat	Keep it up!	Settle down	Slow down
3. Is there a change in pace I can make to increase my progress?					
Physical	❏	❏	❏	❏	❏
Mental	❏	❏	❏	❏	❏
Emotional	❏	❏	❏	❏	❏
Spiritual	❏	❏	❏	❏	❏

The elements of a workout

Positive Thought

Winners work at things that the majority of people are not willing to do.

Dennis Waitley

Practical Tip

Cardiovascular or aerobic fitness, muscular strength, and flexibility are the three components that make up a balanced health and fitness program. Every type of activity that you do will fit into one of these categories. As activity becomes more and more a part of your daily life, ideally you can cross-train, using these three components of fitness during each week.

1. Cardiovascular or aerobic fitness: Any type of activity that is rhythmic and continuous, such as walking, cycling, or swimming, fits into this category. Performing aerobic activity strengthens the heart and lungs, burns calories, and assists in weight control.

2. Muscle strength and endurance: Resistance training or strength training (different names for the same activity) involves making the muscles work harder, and thereby making them stronger. Lifting weights, using elastic resistance, or doing anything that involves pushing, pulling, or lifting will increase your strength and endurance. Muscle strength helps to make all of your activities easier and prevents weakness and injuries as you age.

3. Flexibility: Gentle stretching exercises for the arms, legs, torso, and neck will keep you flexible enough to perform daily activities easily. Because tight muscles can cause discomfort or even contribute to injuries, taking the time for a few gentle stretches each day can also help with stress reduction and relaxation.

Are you doing activities that fall into all three of these categories each week?_____

Balance in your activity schedule will help improve your overall fitness and improve how you feel. List activities that you do that fall into each of these categories:

Aerobic activity

_____

_____

_____

Strength/endurance activity

_____

_____

_____

Flexibility activity

_____

_____

_____

Is there one area that does not have an activity listed? _____ If so, what activity could you do—that you enjoy and find comfortable—in this area? _____

_____

How sweet it is!

Positive Thought

Self-discipline is the process; personal development is the product.

Rhonda H. Kelley
from *Divine Discipline*

Practical Tip

Sugar is one of the most popular foods in our diet. Americans consume an average of 128 pounds of sugar per person each year! Even if you don't intentionally eat sweets, you probably consume more sugar than you think because of all the hidden sugar in processed foods. Sugar comes in a variety of forms, is called by many different names, and is easy to overlook on a package label. Sucrose, fructose, corn syrup, maple syrup, honey, and molasses are all sugars, as are the more familiar white sugar, brown sugar, raw sugar, and powdered sugar.

Often, manufacturers use the word *natural* to try to make you think that brown sugar, raw sugar, and honey are better for you. But did you know that these "natural" sugars have the same amount of calories, and your body doesn't know the difference between natural and processed sugars?

The best "natural" sugar you can eat is contained in fresh fruit. Fructose, the sugar in fruit, is sweeter than sucrose (table sugar), so you are more likely to eat less of it. And in addition, the high water content in fruit makes you feel full faster.

Is sugar bad for you? As with any other food, if you consume sugar in moderate amounts, as part of a balanced, healthy diet, it is not harmful. But there are a number of noteworthy disadvantages to too much sugar:

+ Sugar promotes tooth decay.
+ Sugary foods eaten in excess can promote weight gain because of too many calories consumed.
+ Sugar found in junk foods can replace the nutritious foods in your diet, depriving your body of critical nutrients.
+ The more sweets you eat, the more sweets you seem to crave.
+ Too much sugar may also lead to heart disease.

If you feel that you consume more than a moderate amount of sugar in your diet, there are practical ways to cut back and make your diet healthier.

+ Learn to read package labels and identify products that have less sugar in them.
+ Choose fruit for snacks or dessert instead of candy, cakes, or cookies.
+ Substitute unbuttered popcorn or non-fat pretzels for snacking instead of eating candy or sweets.
+ Drink flavored mineral water instead of soft drinks or sodas (but beware of the high sugar content in certain brands). If you like to drink diet sodas, do so in moderation. The artificial sweeteners and sodium in diet drinks make sodas a less desirable choice than fruit juice or mineral water.
+ Substitute spreadable fruit for sugary jellies and jams.

How can you decrease the amount of sugar in your meals this week? _____

Consider the consequences

Positive Thought

He is no fool who gives what he cannot keep to gain what he cannot lose.

Jim Elliot

Practical Tip

Any choice you make will have an effect or consequence. When you make a positive choice, like eating a healthy snack instead of junk food, you can congratulate yourself on the benefits you are receiving. When you make a negative choice, like watching TV instead of attending your exercise class, you must also accept responsibility for the outcome of that choice. Your goals should be your guide for the choices you make, and the consequences should move you closer toward attaining your goals.

Consider the consequences for your actions:

* Eating a candy bar for a "high energy" snack instead of an apple will increase your calorie intake, diminish the fat-burning potential of your exercise, and may even decrease your energy level.
* Skipping a class will deprive you of the learning you intended to do when you signed up for it.
* Giving up your quiet time for extra sleep will rob you of a peaceful start to your day.
* Watching TV instead of taking an evening

walk with a family member will cheat you of the calorie expenditure you were counting on, and the social time that walking offers.

Every action has a consequence! Concentrate on making positive, healthy choices to gain the positive and healthy benefits that will help you make the lifestyle changes you desire. Soon you will no longer have to struggle to avoid negative choices. Instead, you will view your choices as opportunities to press on consistently toward your goals.

List any negative choices you made this week. What were the consequences of those choices?

Negative choices_____
_____
_____
Consequences_____
_____
_____

Now list the positive choices you made this week. What were the benefits of those choices?

Positive choices_____
_____
_____
Benefits_____
_____
_____

When you are tempted to make a negative choice, think about the consequences and the potential benefits of making a positive choice instead. Let thoughts of those benefits be your motivator to make positive choices more often.

Prayers & Passages

The prudent see danger and take refuge, but the simple keep going and suffer for it.

Proverbs 27:12

Lord, thank you that there are positive benefits to avoiding negative habits. Help me to like the good and healthy choices as much as I have liked the bad! Teach me, I want to learn!
Love,_____

It is your choice!

Positive Thought

When you have to make a choice and don't make it, that is in itself a choice.

William James

Practical Tip

As you pursue the balanced life, you may find it difficult to fit in all of the commitments and changes you have decided to make. Although you set your goals with enthusiasm and the best of intentions, when you assess your progress at the end of the week, you might find your goals were not met. Your reasons might be:

+ I don't have time,
+ It's hard for me to stay motivated, or
+ I've made too big a commitment.

Making lifestyle changes takes time and often may include times of reversal or "backslides." The backslides, though, are a normal part of the growth process. In time, you will learn to schedule your activities in ways that help you keep your commitments. You will adjust your goals to better reflect a commitment that you can handle, and you will find out—by trial and error—what keeps you motivated.

This is a perfect time to be honest with yourself, rather than a victim of excuses. After all, the choices you've made toward a balanced lifestyle are completely yours.

What, if anything, is holding you back from meeting the commitments, choices, or changes you've set for yourself? _____
_____
_____
_____

What can you do today—and in the next few weeks—to move toward those goals?_____
_____
_____
_____

The goals you set are important. Because they are important, make the time and take the time to achieve them!

Journal your thoughts, feelings, joys, and frustrations about your progress: _____
_____
_____
_____
_____
_____
_____
_____

Prayers & Passages

Let us fix our eyes on Jesus, the author and perfecter of our faith.

Hebrews 12:2

Lord, the reminder to focus on you gives me a new perspective. I am confident that you will help me, and knowing that you are working in my life gives me hope. I'm running my race, Lord. Help me to run with perseverance, fixing my eyes on you, the author and perfecter of my faith. Amen.

Facing Challenges

❖ ❖

❖ ❖

❖ ❖

Challenges are something we all face—every day! Week 6 looks at how you perceive challenges and how you can overcome obstacles and solve those challenges.

This week we will explore how to take one step at a time, how to see adversity as an opportunity, and how to make commitments.

Resistance training

Positive Thought

The benefits of resistance training are stronger muscles that:

- *allow you to do every activity with greater ease,*
- *increase your metabolism, burning more calories even when you are at rest, and*
- *help maintain good posture and prevent back pain.*

Practical Tip

By this time, you are well on your way to becoming an active, fit person. You probably feel a difference in your endurance and find that you have more energy to live each day to its fullest potential.

Thus far we have concentrated on simply getting active. The type of activity you choose is not as important as increasing your movement throughout the day. You can and should continue with this philosophy, but if you are ready for an additional challenge, read on!

Resistance training, weight training, strength training, and muscle conditioning are all terms for activities that increase muscle strength and tone. Resistance training doesn't mean that you have to go to a gym and use huge pieces of equipment or enormous dumbbells. It simply means working your muscles a little harder than they're used to. You can use:

- weights,
- your own body weight against gravity,
- machines, or
- anything that adds resistance to a movement.

Resistance exercises should be performed about two times per week to increase and maintain your strength.

If you are ready to add some resistance training into your daily activity schedule, here are two exercises for you to try. You should eventually work up to about twelve to fifteen repetitions of each exercise, but start slowly and do less at first.

Push-ups: Begin in the position of diagram A. Slowly bend your arms and lower your body until your chest almost touches the floor, then press back up into the starting position. Keep your abdominal muscles pulled in so your back doesn't arch. This exercise strengthens and tones the muscles of the chest, the backs of the arms, and the shoulders.

Diagram A:

Back Flye: Begin by sitting on a chair with a pillow on your lap. Lean forward so that you rest the front of your body on the pillow. Holding weights in each hand, let your arms drop down so your hands are near the floor. Keep your elbows slightly bent and slowly lift your arms out to the sides and up until your hands are in line with your shoulders (diagram B). Squeeze your shoulder blades together as you lift your arms. Then slowly lower your arms back to the starting position. This exercise works your upper back and shoulder muscles.

Diagram B:

In future days, we will gradually add resistance exercises for your lower body and abdominals.

Look to the LORD and his strength; seek his face always.

Psalm 105:4

Dear Lord, please help me to apply the discipline I am learning not only to my physical strength, but to my emotional and spiritual strength, as well. Amen.

The peak experience

Positive Thought

Take a chance! All life is a chance. The man who goes farthest is generally the one who is willing to do and dare.

Dale Carnegie's
Scrapbook

Practical Tip

We all face daily challenges. How you perceive a challenge is integral to how you solve that challenge. If you feel that a challenge is overwhelming, then it is going to be difficult to overcome the obstacles you face. But if you determine what the challenge is, then take one step at a time toward solving that challenge, you will usually be successful.

My husband and I [Candice] enjoy mountain climbing. A few years ago, we decided that we would like to set a goal of climbing a 21,000 foot high peak in the Nepal Himalayas. As our technical skills and experience were not sufficient at that time for us to succeed, we spent the next three years taking rock climbing, ice climbing, mountaineering, and first aid classes. We spent every free weekend out in the wilderness, in all kinds of weather, preparing for the challenges we would face.

We finally found ourselves in Kathmandu, Nepal, with a guide and four others who had the same goal that we did. We trekked for three weeks to our base camp at 17,000 feet elevation. The peak suddenly seemed a lot bigger than the pictures in our books. Our guide told us that it would take about nine to twelve hours of climbing to get from our camp to the summit, so we rose at 2:00 a.m. and began. The first couple of hours weren't too difficult, but as we gained elevation it got harder and harder. Roped together in two teams of three people each, we crossed glaciers with crevasses over 100 feet deep. The air at that altitude is so thin that we would take one step, stop and take two breaths, and then take the next step. Instead of being excited about reaching the summit, all I wanted to do was stop and go back to the comforts of base camp.

My challenges were physical, mental, emotional, and spiritual. Each step was difficult, and when we spent three hours climbing a 500 foot vertical wall of ice and snow, I felt like crying and turning back. I couldn't remember why I had ever wanted to do something as crazy as this. I prayed constantly, asking God to just help me go one more step, and to help me stay mentally focused since the safety of my teammates depended on it. When we finally reached the summit, my husband and I felt exhilarated! We had overcome all the obstacles and achieved our goal. It was an equally challenging climb back down, but we made it safely back to base camp fifteen hours after we began.

As I lay in my tent, thankful and exhausted, I pondered the lessons I had learned that day. I realized that taking the challenges one step at a time, knowing that God was there to meet my needs, and focusing on my goals rather than the obstacles was what had led me to success. Whenever I face challenges now, I apply the lessons I learned in the Himalayas to overcome those challenges.

Prayers & Passages

"I tell you the truth, if you have faith as small as a mustard seed, you can say to this mountain, 'Move from here to there' and it will move. Nothing will be impossible for you."
Matthew 17:20

Lord, the obstacles I face seem like mountains. Knowing you are with me, today I make a decision to take just one step. Please take my hand, Lord—and move my mountain! Amen.

ne step at a time

Positive Thought

Adversity causes some men to break; others to break records.

William A. Ward
(1893–1959)

Practical Tip ✦ ✦ ✦ ✦ ✦ ✦ ✦ ✦ ✦ ✦ ✦ ✦ ✦ ✦ ✦ ✦ ✦ ✦ ✦

Keeping in mind yesterday's mountain climbing illustration, let's look at the challenges you might be facing now and what steps you can take to overcome them.

List one challenge that confronts you at this time:

_____

_____

_____

_____

What area of your life does this challenge?
❏ Physical ❏ Emotional ❏ Mental ❏ Spiritual

Why is this a challenge to you? _____

_____

_____

_____

_____

_____

List some steps that you can take, one at a time, to overcome your challenge:

1._____

_____

_____

2._____

_____

_____

3._____

_____

_____

4._____

_____

_____

5._____

_____

_____

6._____

_____

_____

Now take action, beginning with step one. If you take your challenge one step at a time, it will no longer feel so large and intimidating. Rather, it will begin to feel manageable and possible. And as you succeed with each step, you will be more motivated to pursue the next step in your challenge!

Prayers & Passages

God is our refuge and strength, an ever-present help in trouble.

Psalm 46:1

Talk to God about the challenges you face and the steps you know that you need to take. Ask for his guidance. Ask him for courage. Ask him to help you… _____

_____

_____

_____

_____

_____

_____

_____

_____

_____

_____

_____

_____

_____

_____

_____

_____

_____

ommit to it

Positive Thought

We make our decisions, and then our decisions turn around and make us.

F. W. Boreham

Practical Tip

Commitment can be defined as doing, performing, or taking action. It is a pledge or an assurance that you will do whatever it is that you have set out to accomplish. You may often find it easier to let go of a goal or a task rather than commit to it. But commitment is the significant ingredient that moves you forward toward results.

World-class competitive athletes would agree that their minds are a powerful factor in everything they do. To them, learning to commit to goals is as important as training their bodies for competition. Making commitments to your physical, emotional, mental and spiritual goals will help you to take the action necessary to achieve them.

Describe a time in the past when you made a commitment to a person or an action: _____
_____
_____
_____
_____

Describe what you did to keep that commitment (i.e.; how long did it take; what made you decide to do it; who helped you?): _____

_____

_____

_____

_____

_____

_____

Describe how you felt in keeping that commitment:

_____

_____

_____

_____

_____

_____

_____

Making a commitment to someone or something can be a powerful motivator in helping you achieve your goals of a balanced lifestyle.

Prayers & Passages

Commit your way to the LORD; trust in him and he will do this: He will make your righteousness shine like the dawn, the justice of your cause like the noonday sun.

Psalm 37:5–6

Lord, I commit my ways to you today—my hopes, dreams, goals, plans, and desires. I am convinced that without your help, guidance, and intervention in my life, I would not reach the dreams that you have for me. Continue to show me the way. Amen.

Adjust your attitude
to face a challenge

Positive Thought

The pessimist complains about the wind. The optimist expects it to change. The leader adjusts the sails.

John C. Maxwell

Practical Tip

Many different mixtures of personalities make up the human race. Some of us are more naturally optimistic than others. Some of us are more naive than realistic ... and the list of combinations go on and on.

My [Becky] particular personality likes to dream, brainstorm, then do! But inevitably I come up against obstacles and challenges that are strong enough to stop me—if I let them.

Such was the case in 1986 when I was struggling with the decision of whether to keep publishing *My Partner Prayer Notebook* or to let it die. It had been selling slowly, almost coming to a halt, and I needed to evaluate its usefulness. Because I had been doing so much of the work on this project, I felt over-whelmed, disappointed, and defeated. But I was still unwilling to just give up on the book.

Then I heard a motivational sermon called "Let it die or let it fly." As a result, instead of continuing to fret and fear failure, I decided to *do* something.

Freshly inspired, I made phone calls, sent proposals, and eventually found someone who believed in this project and was willing to help me. As a result, *My Partner Prayer Notebook* recently released its tenth anniversary edition!

To this day, inspirational books and tapes are perched on my bookshelf for those inevitable moments when my attitude needs an adjustment, when my courage is weak, or when my personality weaknesses are trying to creep back into my life.

When a challenge seems overwhelming to you, grab your Bible to read, or recite your favorite courage-building Scripture. Or take a long walk or bike ride to clear your mind. Or write out a prayer, pouring out your heart to God. All of these things will help you get through tough times.

What have you done in the past that has helped you to adjust your attitude to face a challenge?

_____

_____

_____

_____

_____

Prayers & Passages

Will the Lord reject forever? Will he never show his favor again? Has his unfailing love vanished forever? Has his promise failed for all time? Has God forgotten to be merciful? Has he in anger withheld his compassion? Then I thought, "To this I will appeal: the years of the right hand of the Most High." I will remember the deeds of the LORD; yes, I will remember your miracles of long ago. I will meditate on all your works and consider all your mighty deeds.

Psalm 77:7–12.

Spend some time meditating on God's mighty deeds in your life.

More challenges...

Positive Thought

If a bird is flying for pleasure it flies with the wind, but if it meets danger, it turns and faces the wind, in order that it may rise higher.

Corrie ten Boom

Practical Tip

You've been working on some of the mental aspects of facing challenges during the last few days. Let's look at our "physical" challenges once again. On Day 1 of this week we began to work on performing upper body resistance training exercises to make your muscles stronger. Today, let's look at three exercises that you can do to make the muscles of your trunk (your abdominal and back muscles) stronger and more toned.

Abdominal Curls: Lie on your back on the floor and interlace your fingers behind your head. Bend your knees so your heels are close to your hips. Take a breath in, and as you exhale lift your head and shoulders off the floor. Try not to pull on your head or neck with your hands. Remember, you only have to lift your shoulders a few inches off the floor in a curl. Don't throw your body and attempt to bring your elbows to your knees. Lower slowly back down until your shoulders touch the floor, breathing in again as you lower. Repeat this curl until you feel fatigue in your abdominal muscles (gradually work up to about twenty-five repetitions).

It's more effective to work slowly, about two seconds up and two seconds down.

Diagram A:

Abdominal Twists: Start in the same position that you did for the curls. As you exhale and begin to curl up, rotate your right shoulder towards your left knee. Lower back down and repeat the curl with rotation to the other side. Make sure it is your shoulder that is twisting toward your knee and not your elbow. Your hands stay behind your head, with your elbows pointing out to the sides. Perform these twists, alternating sides, until you feel fatigue (gradually work up to about twelve on each side). You will feel these in the front of the abdomen and in the waist area.

Diagram B:

Alternating Arm/Leg Raise: Begin by lying on your stomach. Rest your forehead on one arm, and reach over your head with the other arm. Keeping your head down (forehead on arm), lift your right leg and your left arm up off the floor at the same time. The arm and leg will only lift a few inches off the floor. Hold in the "up" position for one to two seconds, and then slowly lower back down to the starting position. Repeat this exercise, lifting your left leg and right arm. Perform about eight to ten repetitions on each side.

Diagram C:

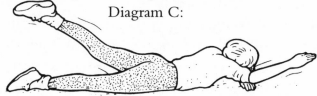

Remember to progress slowly with each of these exercises. If you can only do one to two repetitions at first, that's fine!

Prayers & Passages

But those who hope in the LORD will renew their strength. They will soar on wings like eagles; they will run and not grow weary, they will walk and not be faint.

Isaiah 40:31

Lord, grant me the strength I need to face the challenges in my life—to rise above them, to not grow weary, to walk and not grow faint. Please renew me today. Amen.

Gaining momentum

Positive Thought

Never look back unless you want to go that way.

Susannah Wesley

Practical Tip

You are almost halfway through your 90-day journey, and it's time to chart your progress. At this point, you should feel as if you are gaining momentum and are well on your way to achieving your goals.

Use the chart on the next page to determine how you are progressing in each area. Use the scale of 1–10 and put today's date next to the number you feel is most appropriate. Number one is where you started almost seven weeks ago, and number ten is the point when your goals are achieved in each area.

You may find that you are progressing faster in one area than another. You should see some progress (even a small amount) in each area. If you don't, and are top heavy in one or two areas of your life, you will need to focus a bit more energy in the areas where you are weak.

Remember, charting your progress is meant to keep you on track and motivated. Don't get discouraged if you aren't seeing the progress you expected. Use that discovery to motivate you to make a commitment to work on that area.

PHYSICAL	MENTAL	EMOTIONAL	SPIRITUAL
10	10	10	10
9	9	9	9
8	8	8	8
7	7	7	7
6	6	6	6
5	5	5	5
4	4	4	4
3	3	3	3
2	2	2	2
1	1	1	1
Start date	Start date	Start date	Start date

Pursuing balance is an ongoing process. You should congratulate yourself on having taken the first steps!

Prayers & Passages

I can do everything through him who gives me strength.

Philippians 4:13

Halfway there! Lord, a journey with you on my side to encourage me and guide me is much better than any journey I've done alone. Thank you for your constant presence, your help in the tougher times and the hope you give me to press on. I need you and I love you. Thank you for being the strength of my life. Amen.

PART THREE:

Planning

✦ ✦
✦ ✦
✦ ✦
✦ ✦
✦ ✦

To be consistent and effective in the physical, mental, emotional, and spiritual areas of your life, you need to exercise discipline. In the following three weeks, we will work at eliminating pitfalls, eliminating bad habits, and eliminating excuses.

Eliminating Pitfalls

❖❖
❖❖
❖❖

This week we will tackle the pitfalls that tend to trip us up and impede our progress. Instead of procrastinating, we will prioritize, plan ahead, and press on. With charts and lists, you'll learn to target the traps that tempt you to veer off course. This week could be a real turning point, allowing you to press forward toward your goals.

Plan ahead
or plan to procrastinate

Positive Thought

Most people don't plan to fail; they fail to plan.

John L. Beckley
(1925–)

Practical Tip

In Dennis Waitley's book, *Timing Is Everything*, he says, "Research has concluded repeatedly that a single common denominator of all top performers is this: a clear written focus and *plan*."

In your efforts to make lifestyle changes, one of your greatest accomplishments was to write out your long- and short-term goals, your 90-day goals, and your daily goals. In fact, this would be a perfect time to go back and review your progress since Week 1.

As you look at each of those goals today, has your perspective changed at all?

Long-term goals _____

_____

_____

_____

Short-term goals _____

_____

_____

_____

90-day goals _____
_____
_____
_____

Daily goals _____
_____
_____
_____

For goals to work, they should be flexible, but they also require planning. If you would like to make a change in plans, do so now. Whether you are planning a church event, a child's wedding, a new home, or a return to college, your planning will help you bring your goals to life as you continually break down your goals into smaller-sized goals.

Each day I [Becky] pray about my goals. Through prayer I remember what has yet to be done before I can accomplish my goal, and I ask God to help me in specific ways.

Today, take one goal that has seemed elusive (from Week 1) and break it down into even smaller steps—then take the first step toward achieving it!

This goal has seemed elusive:_____
_____
_____

I will take these steps to achieve that goal:
1. _____
2. _____
3. _____
4. _____

This is what I will do *today* to work toward achieving that goal:_____
_____
_____

"For I know the plans I have for you," declares the LORD, "plans to prosper you and not to harm you, plans to give you hope and a future."

Jeremiah 29:11

Lord, thank you that there is a future and a hope for me—that dreams can turn into goals achieved when I have a plan. Lord, remind me to reach for your plans for my life. Help me day by day. Amen.

Where do you eat?

Positive Thought

If we make it our first goal always to please God, it solves many problems at once.

Philip E. Howard, Jr.

Practical Tip

Planning when, where, and what you are going to eat will help you stick to your commitment of healthy eating. If meals tend to be rushed affairs or you find yourself grabbing a quick bite to eat at your desk at work, in the car, or at a fast-food counter in the mall, then you are a definite candidate for meal-time planning.

For the next day or two, list all of the places where you eat. Examples might be: at the dining room table, over the kitchen sink, in front of the open refrigerator, in the car, as you walk through the grocery store, in a restaurant, on your desk at work, or while you're cooking.

Places Where You Eat	Places You Can Eliminate
1. _____	_____
2. _____	_____
3. _____	_____
4. _____	_____
5. _____	_____

6. _____ _____

7. _____ _____

8. _____ _____

9. _____ _____

10. _____ _____

Now, go back through your list and put check marks by any of the places that trigger bad eating habits such as in your car, where it is possible to eat an entire bag of cookies before you know they are gone, or in the supermarket when you are hungry. Your goal is to reduce the number of places where you eat. Then you should plan when and what you will eat at those places.

Prayers & Passages

"So do not worry, saying, 'What shall we eat?' or 'What shall we drink?' or 'What shall we wear?' For the pagans run after all these things, and your heavenly Father knows that you need them. But seek first his kingdom and his righteousness, and all these things will be given to you as well."

Matthew 6:31–33

Lord, thank you for the food you provide for me to meet my needs. I ask for your help in controlling where I eat and the kinds of food I choose. Help me to grow less preoccupied with food and more in love with you and others. (Add any personal concerns to this prayer.) _____

_____

_____

_____

_____

_____

_____

_____

_____

Satisfying meal times

Positive Thought

Dream dynamic dreams. Let them rise to great goals.

Forge those goals into realistic, workable, time-bound plans.

Dennis Waitley

Practical Tip

Planning where you are going to eat is the first step. Next, look at how you can make your meal times more satisfying, less hurried, and more appropriate. Planning when you are going to eat and what you are going to eat will increase your awareness of food and help you eliminate bad habits.

Most nutrition experts agree that three balanced meals and two to three healthy snacks per day equal a good eating plan for most adults. The formula is ideal, but we want to remind you that ...

1. If you wait to eat until you are starving, you may find that you grab for the quickest foods you can find, rather than the healthier foods you might have chosen if you weren't in such a hurry.

2. If you keep healthy, low-fat snacks handy, you can avoid the excessive hunger that often triggers binges.

3. Keeping a little fuel in your tank all day will keep your energy level steady.

4. Long periods of time between meals can trigger blood sugar reactions that will make you feel

tired, cranky, and more apt to go for that junk food binge.

On the chart below, decide when you would like to have a meal or snack, where you plan to consume it, and what you'd like to eat. Creating a plan or structure will make it easier for you to stick to your goal of healthy eating. You might want to transfer your meal/snack plan to a daybook that you carry with you or to a stick-on memo to put on your calendar. Remind yourself that you have decided to make your eating plan a priority *today*.

When you will eat	Where you will eat	What you will eat
_____	_____	_____
_____	_____	_____
_____	_____	_____
_____	_____	_____
_____	_____	_____
_____	_____	_____

Example:

7:00 a.m. breakfast	Kitchen table with family	Cereal, toast, juice
10:00 a.m. snack	Desk at work	Apple, wheat crackers
12:30 p.m. lunch	Restaurant	Turkey sandwich, salad, mineral water, cookie
3:30 p.m. snack	Kitchen table with children	Raw veggies with yogurt dip, pretzels, juice
6:00 p.m. dinner	Dining room with family	Lasagna, salad, wheat rolls, milk, fresh fruit
8:30 p.m. snack	Den watching TV	Popcorn (no butter)

Eating triggers

Positive Thought

When the passions become masters, they are vices.

Pascal, *Pensees*

Practical Tip

Many situations or places in our lives can trigger eating. Positive triggers include the sight of the family table set for dinner and the smell of a healthy meal in the oven. Negative triggers include fatigue or depression. And some triggers can be either positive or negative, such as parties or other social situations. Being aware of the places or situations that trigger healthy or unhealthy eating for you will help you to change your behavior and find balance in your eating habits.

List all of the places that trigger you to eat. They might include restaurants, your own dining room or kitchen, movie theaters, shopping malls, supermarkets, parties, or a friend's house. Next to them, check whether they are a positive (healthy food) or negative (not so healthy food) trigger. For example, you might list movie theaters as a trigger. If you always eat candy, sodas, and buttered popcorn at the movies, this would be a negative trigger. You might list your favorite restaurant as a trigger, but if you order healthy, balanced meals, it is a positive trigger!

Place that triggers eating	Positive	Negative
_____	_____	_____
_____	_____	_____
_____	_____	_____
_____	_____	_____
_____	_____	_____
_____	_____	_____
_____	_____	_____
_____	_____	_____
_____	_____	_____

Prayers & Passages

No temptation has seized you except what is common to man. And God is faithful; he will not let you be tempted beyond what you can bear. But when you are tempted, he will also provide a way out so that you can stand up under it.

1 Corinthians 10:13

As your awareness increases, you will find it easier to avoid the negative triggers you have identified. Don't overreact though. Just because movies trigger bad eating habits doesn't mean you can't go to the movies anymore. But it does mean that you must plan ahead and take along a healthy snack such as fruit or pretzels. The more negative triggers you can get rid of, the more balanced your eating will be.

Lord, it's happening! I'm thinking differently. I'm recognizing the tempting traps that—in the past—have triggered my bad eating habits. Continue to keep me aware of those places and please give me the courage to stay away from them—until I am no longer tempted. I sure need your help, Lord—every day. Thank you. Amen.

Taking things "litely"

Positive Thought

Experts agree that no more than thirty percent of your total calories should come from fat each day.

Practical Tip

If you are trying to eat a healthy diet, food labels are required reading. Food manufacturers must label packaged foods with a list of ingredients and nutritional information per serving. However, many manufacturers do their best to fool you into thinking that you are eating healthy, low-fat food when you are actually doing just the opposite.

Many foods are labeled "healthy," "lite," "reduced calorie," or "lower-fat." While these labels may tell the truth, they don't tell the whole truth, and the packaging may be misleading. A "healthy" food should include at least three of the following:

- Low in fat, saturated fat, and cholesterol
- Low in sodium
- Low in added sugars
- A good source of nutrients (vitamins, minerals)
- A good source of fiber

Because the nutritional information on labels can be confusing and complex, the Food and Drug Administration is requiring that manufacturers use clear and consistent labeling on all packaged foods.

Here is what you can look for on the labels:

❖ Serving sizes will be consistent across product lines and realistically represent the amounts that people actually eat. When you read a label, you should check to see what the serving size is in relationship to the amount of calories and fat listed. For example, a frozen pizza might say "only 240 calories" on the front of the package. But that serving size may be only 1/4 of the pizza.

❖ The calories per serving, and more importantly the grams of fat and the percentage of calories coming from fat are listed. If you use the same pizza label, that 1/4 of a pizza has 240 calories, 7 g (grams) of fat and 63 of those calories come from fat. If you divide 63 into 240 you will find that 26 percent of your total calories in that pizza are fat. You should select products that have less than 30 percent of the total calories coming from fat.

❖ The amount of saturated fat will be listed as well as the total amount of fat. On your pizza label the saturated fat is listed as 4 g. That means that 4 out of 7 grams of fat in your pizza is saturated. Saturated fat comes from animal products and is the least desirable type of fat to consume in terms of heart disease risk factors (see Week 3, Day 7.)

❖ The amount of dietary fiber is listed. When you are shopping for cereals, crackers, and other grain foods, select one with 2 grams of dietary fiber or more for better nutrition.

❖ The amount of sodium is listed. A reasonable intake of sodium is around 3,000 milligrams per day (the amount found in 1 1/2 teaspoons of salt).

Taking time to educate yourself about good nutrition will result in good health for you and your family.

Prayers & Passages

"And lead us not into temptation, but deliver us from the evil one."
Matthew 6:13

Lord, with your help I'm making an effort to educate myself and change the ways that I think about food. I'm encouraged and ready to make changes in my habits, but I need the strength that only you can give me. Amen.

A matter of fat

Positive Thought

Self-sacrifice through self-control is necessary for self-fulfillment.

Rhonda H. Kelley,
Divine Discipline

Practical Tip

Experts recommend that the average diet should derive thirty percent or less of its total calories from fat. Does that mean that you can't eat any food that contains more than 30 percent fat? Not at all. We're talking about balance here. If you choose to eat a high-fat food at a meal or snacktime, you should try to balance that with a low-fat choice later on. When you look at the total picture, high-fat foods can be part of a healthy, balanced diet if they're compensated for with other low-fat foods. Trying to eliminate all the fat from your diet is not only unhealthy, but will also set you up for eating disorders and other emotional problems associated with denial of food.

To calculate the number of fat calories in a serving of food, multiply the grams of fat per serving by 9 (a gram of fat contains 9 calories), then divide that number by the total calories. For example, if a serving of a frozen meal contains 300 calories and has 10 grams of fat, 90 of those 300 calories come from fat. That's close to one-third of the calories from fat. Another quick way to keep your total fat under 30 percent is to count grams of fat all day. Based on a 2000 calorie per day diet, you should eat under 60 grams of fat per day. Because it's easy to miss hidden fats in foods, you might want to try to keep your fat gram count under 44 grams of fat per day. You may want to familiarize yourself with books such as *The Complete Book of Food Counts* by Corinne Netzer, to learn the fat content of the foods that you eat on a regular basis.

For most people, *watching your fat intake is more important than counting calories.* Use the Food Guide Pyramid (Week 3, Day 7) to make sure you are eating a balanced diet, and use these fat guidelines for both nutritious eating and weight control.

Here are a few simple tricks to cut down on fat:

1. Prepare low-fat snacks like pasta salad, yogurt with fruit, or cut-up vegetables with yogurt dip.

2. Cut in half the amount of butter or margarine you use on food or while cooking. Natural fruit spreads like apple butter are a great alternative to margarine on toast.

3. Spray a pan with vegetable oil spray and stir-fry fish, poultry, and vegetables in fruit or vegetable juice instead of butter or oil.

4. Replace high-fat or whole-milk dairy products (milk, yogurt, cheese, sour cream) with low-fat or non-fat alternatives.

5. Choose lean cuts of meat, poultry, and fish most of the time. Replace regular hot dogs with 94 percent fat-free hot dogs, and remove the skin from chicken and turkey.

Decide on at least one change you can make this week that will make your eating lower in fat and more nutritious.

This week I will _____

_____

_____

Prayers & Passages

My grace is sufficient for you, for my power is made perfect in weakness.
2 Corinthians 12:9

I thank you, Lord, for the abundance of food that I have to choose from. One of my weaknesses is that I am not always as careful to select the foods that are best for me. I pray that you give me the strength to make the better choices and to glorify you through my healthier body.

It's okay to take a break

Positive Thought

If thou may not continually gather thyself together, do it some time at least once a day, morning or evening.

Thomas à Kempis

Practical Tip

As you make commitments to healthy eating and increased activity, remember that moderation is the key to forward progress and momentum. If you plunge headlong into a new activity and require two days of rest to recover from it, your body isn't catching up with its rate of use. If you restrict your diet severely all day and then binge at night, you are creating more stress on your body physically and emotionally. You need time to adapt both physically and mentally to change, and an occasional rest day or a short "time out" within a day can help you to do just that.

A break or rest will often bring freshness back into your routine, making you more responsive to life's demands. Taking a break may mean changing activities, or it may mean doing absolutely nothing! The trick to taking a break is to avoid planning anything specific for that time.

Watch what happens when you have a block of time in your day with nothing scheduled. Sometimes I [Candice] find myself sitting out on my porch with a cup of tea, watching the wind lift the branches of trees up and down. The sound of the wind, the gentle rhythm of the trees, and the sheer pleasure of being able to sit and let my thoughts wander fill me with peace and new energy.

My spiritual life grows, too, when I make time in my schedule for breaks. I find it especially easy to talk with God when I am relaxed and not thinking about the next task on my daily agenda. When I resume my day after a break, things seem clearer, and I am more efficient and focused.

When you take a break, try not to think of all the things you could or should be doing. If you tend to be a "doer" or a busy person by nature, don't let yourself think about that closet you have been meaning to clean out for the last few months, or the letter that you have to write. Try to "take a break" at least a few times each week—if not every day.

In the next day or two, take a break. Record below where you were, what you thought about, and how you felt.

_____
_____
_____
_____
_____
_____
_____
_____
_____
_____

If you regularly include breaks into your day and week, you will feel re-energized, refreshed, and ready for all that life presents!

Prayers & Passages

Be still, and know that I am God.

Psalm 46:10

Lord, teach me to quiet my heart and mind. Teach me the freedom in silence and rest. Help me to slow down enough to hear your voice whispering to me. Cause me to notice your personal touch in the handiwork of the sky and trees and sunshine. Lord, I'm listening …

Eliminating Habits

✦ ✦

✦ ✦

✦ ✦

Habits are patterns of behavior that are acquired over weeks, months, and years. Eliminating old habits and acquiring new habits takes time and practice. Week 8 gives you step–by–step methods to reverse negative habits and replace them with healthy substitutes. In addition, we will examine the quick-fix methods and ruts that have hindered our progress in the past.

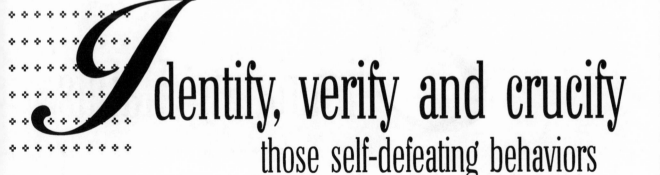

Identify, verify and crucify
those self-defeating behaviors

Positive Thought

Habit is overcome by habit.

Thomas à Kempis

Practical Tip

Habits are defined as patterns of behavior acquired by frequent repetition. They can be acquired over a period of days, weeks, months, or years. Did you know that it is just as easy to develop positive, healthy habits as it is to develop negative, self-defeating ones? For instance, most people practice positive habits of bathing daily and brushing their teeth after meals. Others may practice negative habits such as eating every time they get in a car or choosing to watch TV rather than being active.

This is the week to begin working on turning negative habits into positive habits. In each lifestyle area, identify negative habits that you would like to change and positive habits that you would like to acquire.

For example, in the emotional area of your life you may have the habit of feeling like a victim and complaining about every problem that arises. The positive habit you could acquire might be to face problems optimistically and actively look for solutions. A negative habit in the physical area of your life might be eating a bag of potato chips as you grocery shop. You might want to acquire the habit of shopping only when you're full from a healthy meal.

List below the first "habits" that come to mind in each area.

	Negative habits to change	Positive habits to acquire
Physical		
	_____	_____
	_____	_____
	_____	_____
Mental		
	_____	_____
	_____	_____
	_____	_____
Emotional		
	_____	_____
	_____	_____
	_____	_____
Spiritual		
	_____	_____
	_____	_____
	_____	_____

Take off the blinders

Positive Thought

The recipe for well-being requires neither positive nor negative thinking alone, but a mix of ample optimism to provide hope, a dash of pessimism to prevent complacency, and enough realism to discriminate those things we can control from those we cannot.

David G. Myers,
The Pursuit of Happiness

Practical Tip

What are some steps that you can take to change negative habits? The first step is to recognize what triggers your behavior in each area and what reinforces that behavior. The second step is to eliminate any reinforcements that have shaped that behavior. The final step is to replace negative habits or behaviors with positive ones, and to set positive reinforcements. Let's look at how this can work.

If I decided that one of the negative habits I would like to change is standing over the sink and eating, I need to ask, "What triggers me? Do I eat over the sink when I'm really tired and have had a hard day? I recognize that I tend to skip meals when I'm having a hectic day, and this reinforces my negative behavior of stuffing the first thing I find into my mouth as I stand over the sink."

Step two is to develop a way to avoid skipping meals. If I were not so hungry and tired when I got home, I would be able to take the time to prepare a healthy meal and enjoy it slowly. Therefore, I will commit to packing a healthy lunch and snacks to take with me each day. And I will take a fifteen minute walk on my lunch break so that I will feel less tired and cranky at the end of the day.

My final step is to plan ahead, to make sure that I eat a healthy meal at the dining room table. If I have changed my behavior, I will reinforce it by rewarding myself with dinner at a fun restaurant once a week.

Take one of the negative habits that you would like to change and go through this step-by-step process:

What is a habit you would like to change?_____
_____
_____

What triggers this habit?_____
_____
_____

What reinforces your negative behavior?_____
_____
_____

How can you eliminate these reinforcements?_____
_____
_____

What positive habit can you replace this with?_____
_____
_____

What positive reinforcements can you use to stay motivated to stick with your new behavior?_____
_____
_____

Shifting gears

Positive Thought

To master change, don't press harder on a pedal already floored; shift gears instead.

Ronni Sandroff,
journalist

Practical Tip

A public speaker once said, "You don't have a money problem, you have an idea problem!" I've [Becky] used that bit of advice more than once to prompt me to look for the solution to a financial problem in a different place from where I'd been looking. It prompted me to become active, rather than desperate; to knock on a few new doors, rather than stop knocking.

A radio personality said, "Don't pray about anything you wouldn't want God to do through you." Those words compelled me to stop hoping and praying for someone else to help a friend of mine who was in trouble and to help her myself!

Another convention speaker said, "If you think it's time to quit, it's too soon!" Because of those words, I quit telling myself I should stop working with high-school kids. Instead, I evaluated how I could use my time and talents more effectively and made some needed changes.

Motivation to change gears can come from talking with a friend, memorizing a Bible verse, sharing with a counselor, reviewing a goal list, hearing a song, or reading a motivational book. The key is to have and use those resources to encourage you!

Who is a friend who encourages me?_____
_____
_____

What is a Bible verse that motivates me?_____
_____
_____

Who is a mentor or counselor who gives sound advice?_____
_____
_____

What is on my goal list that reminds me that I am successful?_____
_____
_____

What song lifts my spirits and gives me courage?____
_____
_____

What is a book that causes me to shift gears?_____
_____
_____

Prayers & Passages

It is God who arms me with strength and makes my way perfect. He makes my feet like the feet of a deer; he enables me to stand on the heights.

Psalm 18:32–33

Lord, lift me when I'm low. Show me when to come or go… (add your own heartfelt prayer) _____
_____
_____
_____
_____
_____
_____
_____
_____
_____
_____
_____
_____
_____
_____
_____

Look for healthy substitutes

Positive Thought

Don't windowshop at the bakery.

Carol Weston

Practical Tip

As you shape new behaviors and develop new habits in each area of your life, it's important to find ways to stay accountable to yourself and to your goals. You can keep yourself motivated and accountable by making agreements that state the behaviors that you are trying to eliminate as well as the alternative behaviors you are trying to acquire.

An example of your self-agreement might look like this:

Behavior I wish to change	Substitute behavior
1. I don't want to eat junk food and watch soap operas when I'm bored in the afternoon.	1. I will meet a friend and go for a walk or a bike ride, or I will do volunteer work each afternoon.
2. I don't want to be so angry and short with my family at the end of a long day.	2. I will try to take a "time out" for rest, relaxation, and spiritual renewal each day.

Continue on with your own self-agreement. Try to set one goal and one substitute behavior in each lifestyle area (physical, mental, emotional, and spiritual).

Behavior I wish to change   Substitute behavior

_____   _____

_____   _____

_____   _____

_____   _____

_____   _____

_____   _____

_____   _____

_____   _____

_____   _____

_____   _____

_____   _____

_____   _____

_____   _____

_____   _____

_____   _____

Transfer these to a Post-it note or index card and place them where they can be seen.

Let your eyes look straight ahead, fix your gaze directly before you. Make level paths for your feet and take only ways that are firm. Do not swerve to the right or the left; keep your foot from evil.

Proverbs 4:25–27

Lord, all of life is this way—a series of choices: good or bad, right or wrong, healthy or harmful… Lord, I ask for discernment to make the right choices and determination to do what I have identified as the best for me. As always, I need your help, Lord. Love,_____

Avoid the quick-fix method

Positive Thought

To every disadvantage there is a corresponding advantage.
W. Clement Stone

Practical Tip

Our society values speed and efficiency. We love any kind of machine, gadget, or method that allows us to do something quickly and easily. We see advertisements for a wide range of products, from computers that can process information in seconds to pills that claim to take off excess pounds in a week. With such a barrage of advertising it is easy to fall into the trap of expecting instant results and gratification.

When making lifestyle changes, the "quick-fix method" is not the answer. The benefits you reap are in direct relationship to the time you invest.

If you want to lose weight and create balance in your eating habits, the solution is to make changes gradually in how you eat and how you think about food. This takes time and can only be done by you. No machine, pill, or special food will teach you how to eat moderately and healthfully for the rest of your life. Statistics show that dieting does not work. Deprivation may have short-term benefits in weight loss, but most dieters gain back every pound they lose, plus some, with each diet. Retraining yourself to have healthy eating habits can help you lose weight if you need to, and will certainly make you feel better for a lifetime.

The same is true in each of the other areas of your life. If you want to be fit and healthy, the solution is regular activity. It doesn't matter so much what you do, or how hard you do it, but that you are active consistently. If you want to experience spiritual and emotional growth, you must spend time in the Word and prayer. To nurture mental growth, you must stimulate your mind by expanding your knowledge base. And to grow emotionally you need to take time to learn more about yourself and your feelings.

Take time to journal your thoughts and feelings today:_____

_____

_____

_____

_____

_____

_____

_____

_____

_____

_____

_____

_____

_____

_____

_____

_____

_____

Prayers & Passages

Humble yourselves, therefore, under God's mighty hand, that he may lift you up in due time. Cast all your anxiety on him because he cares for you.
1 Peter 5:6–7

Lord, I want to let go of the anxieties and cares that weigh me down. I ask you to take them from me and help me today to be patient in the process of making lifestyle changes. Help me to make choices that are balanced, rather than quick-fix. And thank you for caring for me, Lord.

Amen.

Reversing the negative

Positive Thought

The good news is... the bad news can be turned into good news... when you change your attitude!

Dr. Robert Schuller,
The Be Happy Attitudes

Practical Tip

Many of the positive and negative habits we fall into are directly related to how we are feeling. I might miss the early evening exercise class I planned to attend because I feel too tired when I get home from work. Or I may sit in front of the TV and eat a carton of ice cream when I'm feeling sorry for myself. Conversely, I find the time for thirty minutes of Bible study and prayer every morning when I am feeling rested, my son is off to school, and the coffee smells delicious.

If you find yourself in a rut and unable to keep the goals you have set for yourself, look at how your emotional state may be effecting your forward momentum. Certain feelings such as anger, frustration, guilt, anxiety, fatigue, unforgiveness, loneliness, or sadness tend to trigger our negative habits. When you feel happy, peaceful, rested, or relieved, you are more likely to practice positive habits.

Once you are aware of how your emotions can trigger negative habits, you can begin to change your cycle of behavior. You can't prevent yourself from experiencing negative feelings, but you can start to avoid the habits that those feelings trigger.

Go back to Day 1 of this week and relist the habits that you would like to change. Next to each habit, write how you tend to feel when you practice this habit.

Negative habit you want to change	Feelings associated with this habit
_____	_____
	_____
	_____
_____	_____
	_____
_____	_____
	_____
	_____
_____	_____
	_____
	_____

Acquire healthy habits

Positive Thought

There is only one corner of the universe you can be certain of improving, and that's your own self.

Aldous Huxley,
Time Must Have a Stop

Practical Tip

Assertiveness in taking responsibility for your feelings and behaviors can lead you to new, positive habits or patterns. If you can re-program yourself to perform a positive activity when you feel certain emotions, you will rid yourself of those negative habits and will be ever closer to your goal of a balanced lifestyle.

List again the emotions you wrote down yesterday—the triggers for negative habits you want to change.

Now, next to each of those feelings, write down one or two positive, creative behaviors that you can do when you feel this way.

Here's an example: One of the feelings I listed was fatigue. When I feel tired, I tend to overeat and be inactive. My creative alternatives are: (1) Take a break and do nothing. This may be a time for mental or spiritual growth, and will probably re-energize me. (2) Get active with a partner. It's easy for me to skip my intended activity session when I have only myself to account to. If I make an appointment with a friend, it won't be easy to back out on my commitment, and I can nurture our friendship as well.

By re-programming my behavior when I feel tired, I am acquiring healthy habits that will take less and less effort to perform as time passes.

Feelings that trigger bad habits	Creative alternatives
_____	1. _____
	2. _____
_____	1. _____
	2. _____
_____	1. _____
	2. _____
_____	1. _____
	2. _____
_____	1. _____
	2. _____
_____	1. _____
	2. _____
_____	1. _____
	2. _____
_____	1. _____
	2. _____

Eliminating Excuses

❖ ❖

❖ ❖

❖ ❖

We've all used excuses: "I'm too tired." "This is too hard." "I'll start tomorrow." But that's no excuse when it comes to making lifestyle changes. Learning to prioritize the important over the urgent will move you forward in leaps and bounds toward your goals. Week 9 gives you practical ways to stay on track when "other" things come up, when you hit plateaus, and when you feel like giving up.

I'll start tomorrow

Positive Thought

Our main business is not to see what lies dimly at a distance, but to do what lies clearly at hand.

Thomas Carlyle

Practical Tip

How many times have you set a goal, had an overwhelming feeling of determination to begin, knew without a doubt that you would achieve your goal—and then decided that you would start tomorrow?

I [Candice] have a lot of unused pieces of sports equipment in my garage that are testimony to my finely tuned skills of procrastination. Here's the typical scenario:

1. I read about a sport or activity, see it demonstrated on TV, and decide with great passion that I must pursue it—my latest being rollerblading.

2. I research all of the equipment that one must have to perform this activity: skates, helmet, knee pads, wrist guards, and a windbreaker that matches my helmet.

3. I convince my husband that we should go to the store and purchase all of this equipment. He gets caught up in the excitement and buys some skates for himself as well. ("This is great!" I think. "We can learn together!")

4. We get home and I put everything on. My husband has something else to do, so I'm on my own.

5. I feel a little silly on the street in front of my house with all this gear and not a clue as to how to get going. Meanwhile, the kid next door flies by on his skates—going backwards!

6. I decide to take it all off and try tomorrow during the day when all the neighborhood kids are in school. I put everything back in the garage in the shopping bag.

7. Tomorrow arrives and I decide to just go for a walk ...

Needless to say, my skates are still in the garage and I am still putting off using them ... until tomorrow. It's a lot easier to procrastinate than to take action.

Try to take action today and do one of those activities that you have been putting off. I'm going to go get those skates on right now!

Do you find yourself putting off commitments until tomorrow? Can you share any action(s) that you have been avoiding? _____

_____

_____

_____

_____

_____

_____

_____

_____

_____

_____

_____

Prayers & Passages

Therefore do not worry about tomorrow, for tomorrow will worry about itself. Each day has enough trouble of its own.

Matthew 6:34

Lord, I have been putting many things off because they are hard, time-consuming, emotionally draining, even painful. Help me today to do just one of those "chores" of mine. Change my heart and mind; give me new thoughts— your thoughts. I need your help, Lord. Amen.

I'm too tired

Positive Thought

Shun idleness. It is the rust that attaches itself to the most brilliant metals.

Voltaire

Practical Tip

Fatigue is often cited as one of the reasons that many people don't accomplish tasks or commitments. Our society looks on busyness and a frenetic lifestyle with admiration. We believe that an important person is busy every waking hour! With this kind of a philosophy, it's no wonder that many of us feel tired more than energized. Do you ever get tired of hearing yourself say how tired you are?

My husband and I [Candice] used to catch ourselves trying to outdo each other with descriptions of how hard our days were. As we have made concerted efforts towards a more balanced lifestyle, we now make it our goal to congratulate each other on finding time for bike rides, for getting our "quiet time" in every day that week, or for completing our tasks by 6:00 p.m. and having the rest of the evening for family time.

If your day is overloaded with work, family, friends, church, or community commitments, then your fatigue is probably very real.

Take a look at all of the roles that you play in a

typical day. Some of them might be: wife, mother, boss, housekeeper, laundress, cook, nurse, friend, entertainer, secretary, etc. Can you eliminate any of the lesser roles in order to make your schedule less frenetic and more balanced and productive? Are the commitments that fill each of your days moving you toward your goals?

In the last few years I have made it a goal to learn to say "no" to some things. I used to feel like I would hurt someone's feelings if I said I couldn't do something they asked of me. But I've found that by being a little more selective with my time, I'm less exhausted and more productive in the areas that I have prioritized as important in my life.

List all of the roles that describe you in a typical day.	Can this be eliminated?
_____	_____
_____	_____
_____	_____
_____	_____
_____	_____
_____	_____
_____	_____
_____	_____
_____	_____

Now go back to "Week 2: Day 1" and look at the five most important things in your life. Put a check mark to the right of the role if it is moving you toward your important goals. What can you eliminate? Place your answer and comment on the line next to the check mark.

When you find yourself saying "I'm too tired," evaluate all of the things that you have said "yes" to, and see if you can re-prioritize your schedule.

Come to me, all you who are weary and burdened, and I will give you rest.

Matthew 11:28

Lord, I've said this over and over. Get me up and out. Help me to go to bed earlier, watch less TV, make less phone calls—whatever it takes—so that I can use my energy more productively. Thank you, Lord.

I can do this alone

Positive Thought

About 15,000,000 people belong to more than 500,000 support groups across the United States.

Practical Tip

Support groups work! If you've ever struggled alone with divorce, depression, bulimia, anorexia, alcoholism, addiction, abuse, disease, death, or unemployment (just to name a few), you do not have to any longer. Of course, you may have to get past the notion that you can fix your problem on your own.

Having struggled with alcoholism and drug addiction, I [Becky] fully understand the shame and guilt attached to such problems. You actually become paralyzed, embarrassed and afraid to let others know about your struggles.

But like millions of other addicts, not until I quit denying my problem, admitted it to others, and asked for help, did I truly begin on the road to recovery.

Yes, it was embarrassing to admit my alcoholism. Yes, I had to change some very comfortable, but unhealthy habits. Yes, I had to admit to family and friends and to God that my life was unmanageable and out of control. And, yes, that is where I began the life-long process of healing.

You can find support groups at a local church, through a Twelve-Step program, or by asking a group of friends who have similar problems to work through a self-help book together.

Being involved in a support group or Twelve-Step group—as a member or as a facilitator—are wonderful ways to keep growing, stay accountable, listen to and encourage others, and be strengthened in your own personal growth—physically, mentally, emotionally, and spiritually.

Along your journey to making lifestyle changes, we want to encourage you to feel good about getting help for yourself.

Prayers & Passages

Therefore confess your sins to each other and pray for each other so that you may be healed. The prayer of a righteous man is powerful and effective.

James 5:16

Pray this prayer if you feel it expresses where you are at this time:

Lord, I do recognize that my life is unmanageable and I can't handle it alone. I need help from you, God. I believe you can help me. I'm asking you to help me. And, Lord, show me where there is a support group for me. Help me not to be afraid. Amen. (This prayer is a paraphrase of the first three steps in the Twelve Steps of Alcoholics Anonymous.)

Something important
has come up

Positive Thought

The reason most major goals are not achieved is that we spend our time doing second things first.

Robert J. McKain

Practical Tip

Research has shown that one of the excuses of people who have dropped out of an exercise program is, "Something came up, and I didn't have time." Learning to prioritize the important over the urgent will move you forward in leaps and bounds toward your goals.

Scheduling in your priorities will help ensure that they don't get scheduled out by things that "come up." The trick is to make your personal priorities just as important as a business meeting or a doctor's appointment. Think about the things that never get pushed off your schedule. What is it that makes them important enough to you that they are prioritized in your day? Can you make your activity, your healthy meal, your reading time, or your prayer time just as important?

What are some of your priorities that tend to get pushed out of your schedule by "something that came up?" List them below and in the next week, see if you can "re-schedule" them so that they don't get pushed aside. Check them off when you do achieve them.

Priorities that get pushed off my schedule	Time & Day Rescheduled	Achieved
_____	_____	_____
_____	_____	_____
_____	_____	_____
_____	_____	_____
_____	_____	_____
_____	_____	_____
_____	_____	_____
_____	_____	_____
_____	_____	_____
_____	_____	_____
_____	_____	_____
_____	_____	_____
_____	_____	_____
_____	_____	_____
_____	_____	_____
_____	_____	_____
_____	_____	_____
_____	_____	_____
_____	_____	_____
_____	_____	_____
_____	_____	_____

Prayers & Passages

He who works his land will have abundant food, but he who chases fantasies lacks judgment.

Proverbs 12:11

A sluggard does not plow in season; so at harvest time he looks but finds nothing.

Proverbs 20:4

Lord, I genuinely struggle with this area of priorities. I have a hard time knowing what is urgent and discerning when to say "no." Please, Lord, help me daily to discover my most important priorities—and then *do* them!

Write a personal prayer, detailing your specific struggles… _____
_____
_____
_____
_____
_____
_____
_____
_____

I'll never get there

Positive Thought

Slow and steady wins the race.

Aesop,
"The Hare and
the Tortoise"

Practical Tip

Sometimes progress seems slow, and we become discouraged in the process of reaching our goals. That feeling of "I'll never get there" can be strong enough to send us into a backslide, to stall us—or to even stop us altogether!

Be patient. Remember, it takes time to see and feel measurable results even when you are making forward progress in your efforts. The amount of time that it takes to see and feel results in each lifestyle area will depend on:

1. how much change you are trying to make in that area, and

2. how much time you are investing in those changes.

Refer to the chart on the following page to see whether you are making progress. Congratulate yourself for any sign of healthy progress toward your goals.

When you have the feeling "I'll never get there," remember that patience, trusting in God, and persistence will get you there!

	What you may feel	What you may see
Physical improvement		
Activity	More energized right away. Stronger and more fit in about 4–6 weeks.	After about 4–6 weeks you may start to look leaner and see toned muscles.
Healthy Eating	More energized right away. Less desire for "junk food" after a few weeks of good habits.	After about 3–4 weeks you may see some weight loss and clearer skin. After 3–4 weeks your refrigerator and cupboards will contain healthier foods.
Mental Growth	More focused right away. Sense of determination.	More organization on desk area. Catching up with correspondence and/or bill paying.
Emotional Growth	Less anxiety. More in control of your life.	Less compulsive behavior. Less binge eating or other obsessive habits.
Spiritual Growth	A greater sense of peace right away. A stronger relationship with God after a few days.	A difference in your temperament (i.e., less anger). Quiet times finding their way into your daily routine.

Prayers & Passages

Consider it pure joy, my brothers, whenever you face trials of many kinds, because you know that the testing of your faith develops perseverance. Perseverance must finish its work so that you may be mature and complete, not lacking anything.

James 1:2–4

Lord, I'm not very patient. I often give up before I've achieved my goal. Sometimes I feel as if it will never happen and I get genuinely discouraged. Help me in this 90-Day journey *not* to give up, give in, quit, or stop trying. I need your help, Lord, to get there. Thank you.

I've hit a plateau

Positive Thought

Sight and feelings are hindrances to believing and trusting God.

Charles Stanley

Practical Tip

Perhaps you've experienced this scenario: You've been working hard at your goals, you've seen progress, then all of a sudden you feel as if you are on a treadmill and going nowhere. In any new endeavor, you will see a lot of progress at the outset, but that rate of progress will decrease. This does not mean you're doing something wrong; in fact, your progress will naturally fluctuate as you move toward change. The trick is to recognize when you have hit a plateau in a lifestyle area, and do one of two things:

1. Just relax and know that this won't last forever. Hold firm and continue doing what you are doing, knowing that your forward momentum will probably resume again soon.

2. Change what you are doing, or let the new stimulus move you forward again. Sometimes hitting a plateau is a sign that you need change.

If you have increased your activity level but are doing the same thing every day, you might want to change activities and, in essence, shock your body into change again. If, for example, you have been walking for thirty minutes every other day, you may want to change your activity to cycling or another recreational sport on an alternate day. Or you may want to vary the intensity of your activity sessions by walking faster one day, slower the next, and longer on another day.

You can change the stimulus in the other areas of your life as well. Try a healthy recipe that you haven't attempted yet, or change the way you structure your spiritual time by picking up a new devotional that allows you to study a familiar Scripture in a new way.

Is there an area of your life in which you feel that you've hit a plateau? _____
_____
_____
_____
_____
_____

What can you do to stimulate yourself by creating change in this area? _____
_____
_____
_____
_____
_____

Remember, you have the freedom to create small or large changes in your routine—at any time! Just because you cannot see or feel a change at this very moment does not mean it's not right around the corner!

This is just too hard

Positive Thought

When the going gets tough, the tough get going.

Anonymous,
popularized by John N.
Mitchell, attorney general
under Richard Nixon

Practical Tip

We all have days when everything seems like too much effort. On those days we may complain, "It's just too hard." Making change is hard and takes a considerable amount of effort and endurance on your part. If—and when—you have one of those "hard" days, here are a few things you can do:

1. Write down all of the benefits you gain from your efforts. A recent research report from the Human Nutrition Research Center on Aging at Tufts University stated that the body's decline is due not to the passing of years, but to the combined effects of inactivity, poor nutrition, and illness... much of which can be controlled! Whenever you fall into a slump with exercise and eating, go back and read quotes like this and make a list of all the benefits that you see and feel for your efforts. Take advantage of the many great motivational books, tools, and quotes that are intended to get you through tough spots.

2. Congratulate yourself on your efforts so far. Sometimes we get so caught up in making progress

that we forget to give ourselves credit for what we've accomplished!

Write down a few sentences describing the positive efforts you have made this week. _____
_____
_____
_____

3. Keep a record of your progress. In each lifestyle area, keep a daily log of all the things you do—no matter how small! If you ...
+ take the stairs instead of the elevator,
+ ask for your pasta to be prepared without oil at a restaurant, or
+ find ten minutes to read your Bible

Write it down!

+ _____
_____
+ _____
_____
+ _____
_____

You may be surprised at the ease of your progress and motivated by seeing how much you have accomplished!

4. Make a list of the easier tasks that you can do in each lifestyle area, then check them off as you accomplish them. You will notice a great sense of satisfaction in checking those tasks off that list! During a difficult time choose the easiest route to your goals, taking one step at a time.

Not only so, but we also rejoice in our sufferings, because we know that suffering produces perseverance; perseverance, character; and character, hope. And hope does not disappoint us, because God has poured out his love into our hearts by the Holy Spirit, whom he has given us.

Romans 5:3–5

Lord, I am encouraged when I read these verses in Romans—that suffering builds my character, gives me hope, and causes me to endure. I am so glad, too, to know that you pour out your love to me through the Holy Spirit! Thank you, that when life—and its tasks—seem too hard, I can look to you for strength and courage and hope. I love you, Lord.

Achievement

You have succeeded in set-ting your goals, getting motivated, and planning ahead. Now you are ready to celebrate your achievements and continue to work on lifestyle changes. The next few weeks, you will pursue health, happiness, hope, and peace.

Pursuing Health

❖ ❖
❖ ❖
❖ ❖

By this time we hope that you have found that increased activity and healthy eating have made positive changes in your life. Throughout this week, we will continue to give you creative and fun ideas to take your health and fitness to new levels. You will learn to make exercise a family affair, fine-tune your eating awareness, and strengthen your muscles in this exciting, action-packed week!

Back to basics

Positive Thought

No one knows what he can do till he tries.

Publius Syrus,
Moral Sayings

Practical Tip

Back pain is a very common complaint. In fact, up to seventy percent of us will experience problems or pain in our backs at some point in our lives. Some people experience chronic, low-grade pain, and others experience a sudden onset of pain with a simple action such as picking up a baby.

Because back pain is a problem that can usually be prevented, let's look at some of its causes and what you can do to avoid this complaint.

Back injuries are occasionally caused by a single, painful incident. But usually, they are caused by a gradual accumulation of poor posture, inactivity, weak muscles, lack of flexibility, stress, and improper lifting techniques.

Use the following chart to determine if you are at risk for back problems. If you check "needs improving" in any area, you may be at risk for back problems.

	Good	Fair	Needs Improving
How is your posture throughout the day?	❏	❏	❏
How consistent is your activity or exercise?	❏	❏	❏
How strong are your abdominal muscles?	❏	❏	❏
How is your flexibility (in your lower back, calf muscles, and the back of your thighs)?	❏	❏	❏
How do you rate your bending and lifting techniques?	❏	❏	❏

Here are some helpful hints to improve your back health.

1. Practice good posture all day. Avoid slumping while you are standing, sitting, or moving. Using a lumbar support like a pillow or rolled-up towel can help you maintain good posture when you have to sit for long periods of time in the car or office.

2. Strengthen your abdominal and back muscles. Strong muscles help support the back and make it easier to maintain good posture. Use the exercises on Week 6, Day 6.

3. Stretch regularly. Tight muscles can cause poor posture. Lie on your back and pull one knee in at a time to your chest to stretch your lower back. Relax and hold the stretch for ten seconds. To stretch the back of the thighs, lie on your back and pull one knee in toward your chest. Then, interlace your fingers around the back of your thigh and slowly straighten your knee until the bottom of your foot is facing the ceiling. Repeat with the other leg. You shouldn't feel any pain as you stretch.

4. Use your legs, not your back, to lift heavy objects. Bending over from the waist to pick something up is a good way to injure your back. Always bend your knees, tighten your abdominal muscles, keep your chest up, and use your leg muscles to lift the object.

Prayers & Passages

The LORD is the strength of my life—of whom shall I be afraid?
Psalm 27:1 (NKJV)

Lord, strengthen me today—physically, mentally, emotionally, and spiritually. Be the strength of my life! Amen.

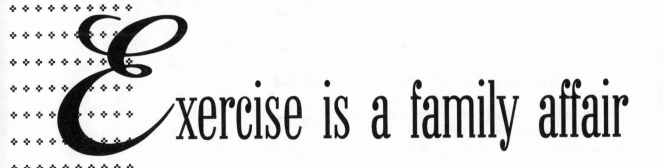

Exercise is a family affair

Positive Thought

This habit of uselessly wasting time is the whole difficulty; it is vastly important to you, and still more so to your children, that you should break the habit. It is more important to them, because they have longer to live, and can keep out of an idle habit before they are in it, easier than they can get out after they are in.

Abraham Lincoln

Practical Tip

By this time we hope that you are being consistent with your increased activity and exercise. A great way to *stay* motivated is to make activity a family affair. Family could include your spouse and children, or your parents, brothers and sisters, or other relatives or your roommates. Good health and fitness as a lifestyle will be easier to maintain if you have the support of those closest to you.

Here's our formula. FIT equals:

F – Families
I – Improving
T – Together

Besides helping you to stay fit, family activity is a good way to prioritize and nurture your family relationships. You may find double payoff for your efforts as your family grows closer and healthier!

Finding activities that appeal to all members of the family can be difficult, especially if you have a large range of ages and interests. Try to let family members take turns choosing the activity in which you will all participate. Activities can range from quick twenty-minute play sessions to all-day outings. Here are some suggestions that we've tried with our families:

- A hike in a state park that ends with a picnic lunch.
- A bike ride to the beach for a cookout and volleyball game.
- A game of hide-and-seek in the house and yard.
- Softball at the local park or school.
- Relay races in a neighborhood pool or lake.
- Swinging and playing tag at the park or playground.
- Ice skating or roller skating/blading.

The activity you choose is not as important as the time you spend as a family with the goal of being active, healthy, and together! Today—or sometime this week—have a little family meeting. Discuss with each person in your family what it is they like to do. Then put some dates, times, and activities on your calendar!

Write down a few of the family times you all came up with:

What	Where	When
_____	_____	_____
_____	_____	_____
_____	_____	_____
_____	_____	_____
_____	_____	_____
_____	_____	_____
_____	_____	_____

Prayers & Passages

There is a time for everything, and a season for every activity under heaven.
Ecclesiastes 3:1

Take time to pray about each area of your life: physical fitness, emotional and mental growth, and spiritual health._____
_____
_____
_____
_____
_____
_____
_____
_____
_____
_____
_____
_____

A strong foundation

Positive Thought

There are three ways that prepare us for life's trials. One is the Spartan way that says, "I have strength within me to do it, I am the captain of my soul. With the courage and will that is mine, I will be master when the struggle comes." Another way is the spirit of Socrates, who affirmed that we have minds, reason, and judgment to evaluate and help us cope with the enigmas and struggles of life. The Christian way is the third approach. It doesn't exclude the other two, but it adds, "You don't begin with yourself, your will or your reason. You begin with God, who is the beginning and the end."

Lowell R. Ditzen

Practical Tip

We've talked about the fact that strength or resistance training helps develop strong muscles. The other good news is that as you get stronger, your body is able to burn more calories, not only when you are active, but also when you are at rest.

Toning the muscles in your legs and hips will give you a strong foundation and should make all weight-bearing activities and chores easier. The following three exercises are for the large muscle groups of the hips and legs.

Parallel Squat: Stand with both hands on the back of a chair for balance. Your feet should be about shoulder distance apart, with your toes pointing straight ahead or turned out slightly. Keeping your abdominal muscles pulled in and your heels on the floor, slowly bend your knees. Your weight should be in your heels and your hips should go back as if you were trying to sit down in a chair. Make sure that your knees do not go forward and past your toes. They should stay aligned over the middle of the foot. Lower until your hips are almost in line with your knees, and then slowly lift back to your starting position. Bend only as low as is comfortable for you, but no deeper than the point where your thighs are parallel to the floor. Perform twelve to twenty repetitions of this exercise at least twice each week. This exercise helps strengthen and shape the muscles of the hips and thighs.

Diagram A:

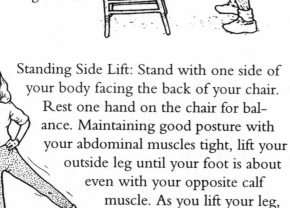

Standing Side Lift: Stand with one side of your body facing the back of your chair. Rest one hand on the chair for balance. Maintaining good posture with your abdominal muscles tight, lift your outside leg until your foot is about even with your opposite calf muscle. As you lift your leg, your knee and toe should point forward. Do not turn the knee and toe up to face the ceiling. Lower your leg slowly

Diagram B:

back to the starting position. Perform twelve to twenty repetitions of this exercise twice each week. As you get stronger you may add one- to three-pound ankle weights if you desire. This exercise helps strengthen and shape the outer part of the hips and thighs.

Hamstring Curl: Lie on the floor face down with one ankle crossed over the other one. Rest your chin on your hands and keep your abdominal muscles pulled in. Bend your knees and curl your heels in towards your hips. As you bend your knees, the leg on top creates resistance by pushing down on the leg on the bottom. In other words, your top leg becomes a weight for the bottom leg to lift. Perform twelve to twenty repetitions of this exercise twice each week. This exercise helps strengthen and shape the backs of the thighs.

Diagram C:

169

Note:
non-foods can fool you

Positive Thought

Your capacity to say no determines your capacity to say yes to greater things.

E. Stanley Jones

Practical Tip

Condiments and other "non-foods" can fool you! You might think you are eating a healthy diet because you can use them without really thinking, but condiments often have as many, if not more calories than the foods on which we use them.

Beware! These "non-foods" could be making up a considerably larger portion of your total calorie intake than you realize. Many condiments are high in fat and cholesterol, which can outweigh the benefits of the low-fat foods you are putting them on.

Here's an example: Your dinner consists of a large piece of grilled fish, a fresh whole wheat roll and a salad with lots of fresh vegetables. You "enhance" those foods with a heaping tablespoon of tartar sauce on your fish, a tablespoon of butter or margarine on your roll, and three tablespoons of Thousand Island dressing on your salad. You have just about doubled the calories of your dinner with those added condiments. Better choices might be: fresh lemon squeezed on your fish, light vinegar and olive oil dressing on your salad, and lowfat spread for your wheat roll.

The following is a list of calorie counts for the more common condiments. Become familiar with the calories in them so you can wisely choose which to use, which to use sparingly, and which to avoid.

Just eliminating most of the higher calorie condiments from my [Becky's] meals over the last year has caused my weight to fluctuate less. Because I've already decided what foods and what condiments are worth their calorie and fat content to me, I have decided in advance to prepare foods without mayonnaise and in restaurants to ask for dressing on the side.

	Calories per tablespoon
Butter or margarine	102
Oils (corn, safflower, olive, peanut)	120
Mayonnaise	100
Tartar sauce	70
Cream cheese	100
Creamy blue cheese dressing	80
Thousand Island dressing	60
Jams and jellies	40
Fruit spreads (no added sugar)	8
Cream	52
Half and half	20
Catsup	16
Mustard	16

As you choose condiments, be aware of the amounts that you use and ask yourself if the amount of taste you are getting is really worth the extra calories and fat. You may be surprised to find out how tasty your food really is without them!

Take time to take action

Positive Thought

Saying is one thing and doing is another.

Montaigne, *Essays*

Practical Tip

It's time to check in and take a progress report. Do you remember the chart that you filled out on Week 1, Day 1? Don't turn back to it quite yet! First, fill out the chart on the following page and assess the overall level of activity that you are doing up to this point.

Just like you did before, determine what it is that you are usually doing for each two-hour block of the day. Using the Activity Level Guide, rate that time slot as a "low," "medium," or "high" activity level. Give yourself one point for each low activity level block, two points for each medium activity level block, and a big three points for each high activity level block. Total your points. Now go back to Week 1, Day 1 and look at the chart you filled out ten weeks ago. Hopefully you have increased your activity level and earned more total points! Congratulate yourself if you have made any improvement. If you feel that you still need improvement, use this chart every eight to ten weeks to assess your progress.

Remember, speed of progress isn't as important as (1) making gradual changes in your activity level, and (2) being honest regarding the changes that you should make.

Low: Sedentary or little activity
- ❖ sleeping
- ❖ watching TV
- ❖ driving
- ❖ reading/studying

Medium: Busy around home or work
- ❖ housework/shopping
- ❖ gardening
- ❖ moving around office
- ❖ running errands

High: Vigorous activity or exercise
- ❖ brisk walking
- ❖ any sport or aerobic activity that is vigorous for at least 15 minutes at a time

	LOW	MEDIUM	HIGH
6am–8am			
8am–10am			
10am–12pm			
12pm–2pm			
2pm–4pm			
4pm–6pm			
6pm–8pm			
8pm–10pm			

Totals: _____   _____   _____

- ❑ I feel good about my activity level.
- ❑ I would like to make a few changes in my activity level.
- ❑ I absolutely need to make changes in my activity level.

Prayers & Passages

His master replied, "Well done, good and faithful servant! You have been faithful with a few things; I will put you in charge of many things. Come and share your master's happiness!"

Matthew 25:21

Lord, cause me not to seek only physical goals, but to balance my life by putting you first. Help me to be faithful to you in all things. Love, _____

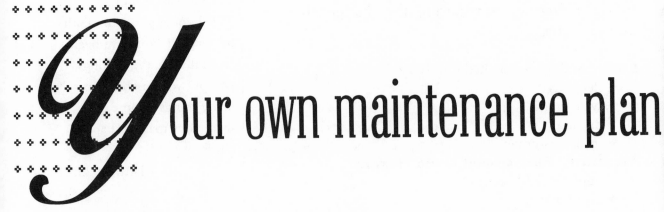

Your own maintenance plan

Positive Thought

*Take charge of your life!...
To act intelligently and effectively, we still must have a
plan. To the proverb which
says, "A journey of a thousand
miles begins with a single
step," I would add the words
"and a road map."*

Cecile M. Springer

Practical Tip

Healthy eating and regular activity can add years
to your life. They will definitely also add life to
your years! Research now shows that the effects of
aging can be slowed down and even reversed, no
matter how old you are or how long you've
neglected your body in the past.

Therefore, if you haven't done anything yet, you
now have a second chance to rejuvenate and regain
your energy, health, and vitality.

Americans spend millions of dollars every year
trying to "undo" the damage they have done to
themselves with poor eating habits and inactivity.
Statistics show that major killers such as heart disease and cancer could largely be prevented by activity and moderate low-fat eating. Prevention is
simple, inexpensive, and can save you pain and
money. A small investment of time on a daily basis
can change your life—and even *save* your life.

Overcome that lurking tendency toward inaction
by tracking your progress on a daily basis. If you
find that you are reverting to your old sedentary

ways, use the following checklist to get back on track.

Have I done some kind of activity or exercise today?
Yes   No

If not, what was my excuse for avoiding it? _____
_____

What activity do I plan to do tomorrow? _____
_____

What are the benefits I will receive from being active? _____
_____

Have I eaten healthy, balanced meals and snacks today?   Yes   No   If not, what triggered my negative behavior? _____
_____

What can I do tomorrow to get back on track? _____
_____

What are the benefits I've seen so far from healthy eating? _____
_____

How do I feel when I'm taking good care of myself? _____
_____

To help you stay on track, make a copy of this checklist or commit it to memory. An effective "maintenance plan" helps you make lifestyle changes that will last a lifetime.

Prayers & Passages

"I am the vine; you are the branches. If a man remains in me and I in him, he will bear much fruit; apart from me you can do nothing."

John 15:5

Lord, perhaps this struggle with my body—the disciplining of my mind and the self-control of my flesh—is helping me to grow spiritually. Saying no to myself, making time for what is truly important, and developing integrity are what I am really striving for. I can't do it without you, Lord. Amen.

Making your lifestyle food friendly

Positive Thought

There is one exception to the rule "Never eat at a restaurant called Mom's." If you're in a small town, and the only other place is called Eats—then go to Mom's.

Carl Waxman

Practical Tip

The classic American diet is typically high in sugar, refined flours, saturated fats, and protein. Knowing that this type of diet is linked to heart disease, obesity, high blood pressure, diabetes, and colon cancer, we shouldn't need much more motivation to eat healthy, balanced meals.

In countries where diets are lower in fat and higher in complex carbohydrates and fiber, the mortality rate from heart disease and obesity-related disease is much lower. Let's take a look at each of the vital components of a well balanced diet.

Carbohydrates: The largest percentage of your total calories should come from carbohydrates. These are the foods that are broken down into glucose, which is the main fuel your brain and muscles use. In addition to supplying energy, carbohydrate foods such as whole grains, beans, fruits, and vegetables also supply vitamins, minerals, and dietary fiber. They should make up about sixty-five percent of a good, low-fat diet. Some of the advantages of carbohydrates are that they are not too fattening.

they satisfy your psychological need to chew and feel full, they can satisfy a sweet tooth (fruit), and they help you increase your intake of important dietary fiber.

Protein: Most Americans eat about twice as much protein as they really need for good nutrition, and many of the sources of protein are high in both calories and fat. Our bodies use broken-down protein to form new tissues, transport nutrients, make antibodies to help us fight disease, and perform many other vital functions. About forty to sixty grams of protein a day—or about twelve percent of your total calories—is recommended for the average adult. Good, low-fat sources of protein are lean meats and poultry, fish, eggs, low or non-fat dairy products and vegetable proteins (such as combinations of beans or legumes and rice.)

Fat: Although fat is an essential nutrient, much of the fat we eat is unnecessary for good nutrition. Dietary fat helps transport fat-soluble vitamins into your body and helps you absorb vitamins A, D, and E. Fat is also a concentrated source of energy in your body, and it makes foods taste good. Since fats supply nine calories per gram (as compared to four calories per gram from carbohydrates and protein), the key is to limit the amount and types of fat in your diet. Less than thirty percent of your total calories should come from fat, and you would be wise to eat less saturated animal fat, less cholesterol, and more polyunsaturated vegetable fats.

Water: This most vital nutrient is the one that is most neglected. Your body is about two-thirds water, and every cell in your body depends on water to function. Water is essential for the digestion and absorption of food, the elimination of digestive wastes, and the regulation of your body

Prayers & Passages

"Watch and pray so that you will not fall into temptation. The spirit is willing, but the body is weak."

Matthew 26:41

Lord, through this journey I have truly recognized that I fight my flesh when I allow your Spirit to renew my mind. What a challenge! Daily renew my mind, O Lord. I need your help. Thank you!

temperature. The best news about water is that it has no calories and you can have as much of it as you want! You should consume about six to eight glasses of liquid a day (more in hot weather), and eat plenty of fruits and vegetables, which have high water content.

Use the Food Guide Pyramid (Week 3, Day 7) along with this nutrient guide to evaluate your diet today. See if you are eating a balanced diet from all the food groups. List the types of food you ate and the number of servings in each group. (Before you fill out this chart, you may want to photocopy it for future use.)

Carbohydrates

Grain Group _____

Vegetable Group _____

Fruit Group _____

Proteins

Milk, Yogurt, Cheese Group _____

Meat, Poultry, Fish, Nuts, Eggs Group _____

Fats

Fats, Oils, Sweets Group _____

Water

How many glasses? _____

Other liquids _____

Pursuing Happiness

✦ ✦

✦ ✦

✦ ✦

We have come to realize in our lives that happiness is achievable when our lives are balanced physically, mentally, emotionally, and spiritually. In this week, you will discover that happiness comes from being willing to forgive others, accepting yourself, finding contentment in all situations, and giving of yourself. Our focus will turn from the outer person to the inner person.

"I would be happy if..."

Positive Thought

You will become as small as your controlling desires ... as great as your dominant aspiration.

James Allen

Practical Tip

Happiness can be elusive if you do not know exactly what will make you happy. It is easy to look in a mirror and think that a change in your appearance would make the difference between happiness and unhappiness. Do you focus on your physical self and think, "I would be happy if I were thinner... or prettier... or had different hair?"

It is also easy to compare yourself to others and think that you would be happy if some mental or emotional aspect of your life was different. Do you focus on your personality and think "I would be happy if I were smarter ... or funnier ... or more outgoing?"

Take a moment to journal your thoughts on what you think would make you happy. _____
_____
_____
_____
_____
_____

Accepting and loving yourself *as you are today* is an important step in finding true happiness. If you can find ways to look at the positive aspects in both your outer and inner self, you will begin to feel the happiness that self-acceptance can bring.

Review today's journal entry. To practice seeing happiness in *today,* write down what makes you happy about yourself physically, mentally, emotionally, and spiritually. For example, if you wrote down on the previous page that getting thinner would make you happy, you might now write that God made you in his image—and you should feel awe in that knowledge! Remembering that God loves you just the way you are today makes it easier to love and accept yourself.

Write down a positive attribute in each area of your life:

Physical_____

_____

_____

Mental_____

_____

_____

Emotional_____

_____

_____

Spiritual_____

_____

_____

Prayers & Passages

Delight yourself in the LORD and he will give you the desires of your heart.
Psalm 37:4

Lord, continually give me your perspective on life and living. Remind me, especially when I'm feeling unhappy, how many blessings I really do have, how much you care for me, and how special I am to you. I have constantly struggled with accepting myself. In light of your Word and your love for me, cause me to feel the happiness that comes from knowing that you love me.
Love,_____

Giving gives ...

Positive Thought

Find a need and fill it.
Ruth Stafford Peale
(1906–)

Practical Tip

Some of my happiest childhood memories are from holidays like birthdays and Christmas where gifts were exchanged. I [Candice] remember feeling almost sick with excitement at the anticipation of unopened presents. As I got a little older I felt the same feeling when someone was opening a present that I had carefully made and wrapped. In fact, that feeling I got from giving presents was almost better than the feeling I got from getting them.

Giving is a great way to pursue happiness. Instead of thinking about what would make you happy, think about what would make someone else happy.

Giving gives life. Think of the Dead Sea, a large body of water situated between Israel and Jordan. The Dead Sea receives a heavy inflow of fresh water from the Jordan River and several smaller streams. But because it is nearly six times as salty as the ocean, and does not have an outlet, it cannot support life. Even fish put into its water soon die. With no outlet to give any of its water away, the Dead Sea lacks life. In the same way, a person's human growth and development will stagnate if it only receives and never gives.

Giving gives back to the giver! Consider this challenge: try giving in the area(s) that you are the least satisfied with in your personal life:

❖ If you have trouble getting and staying active, you might volunteer at a nursing home to take wheelchair patients outdoors for a walk. By this service, you will get your exercise while bringing joy into someone's life.

❖ If you tend not to be generous, sponsor a child through an organization that gives food, medical, and educational support. Each month when you write your check, think about how fortunate you are to be in the position where you can write a check. It may mean a small sacrifice for you, but the recipient will be greatly blessed!

❖ If you have difficulty with overeating and struggle to diet, think about working once a week at a food kitchen for homeless people. Giving food away may give you a new perspective on hunger.

❖ If you have been attending church for years, but have never volunteered, sign up to teach vacation Bible school, baby-sit in the nursery, or lead a Bible study.

How can you "give" in a new way? _____
_____
_____
_____
_____
_____

Prayers & Passages

In everything I did, I showed you that by this kind of hard work we must help the weak, remembering the words the Lord Jesus himself said: "It is more blessed to give than to receive."

Acts 20:35

Lord, I am often so concerned about myself, my needs, and my goals that I have overlooked many opportunities for giving, helping, and serving others. Lord, I do know of a few needs that I could fill—and even enjoy filling! Open my heart to want to help; open my hands to offer my services. Amen.

Untrapped

Positive Thought

Never cease loving a person, and never give up hope for him, for even the prodigal son who had fallen most low, could still be saved; the bitterest enemy, and also he who was your friend could again be your friend; love that has grown cold can kindle again.

Søren Kierkegaard

Practical Tip

Have you ever been hurt by someone close to you? My [Candice's] friend Laurie was betrayed by her friend and co-worker, Amanda, and lost a promotion she deserved. Four years later she still speaks with anger about her friend's betrayal. She feels tension every day at work because she purposely avoids speaking to Amanda. And her friendships with other co-workers have been compromised because they try to avoid taking sides with either woman. As this example shows, guilt and resentment can actually intensify over time. If you do not forgive, releasing those negative feelings of anger and resentment, you will be hindered from moving forward with your life.

Guilt or self-hatred can also fill you with hurt, keeping you from accepting and loving yourself. Are there things in your past that you haven't forgiven yourself for? Holding on to negative emotions can block your ability to feel joy. They may also hold you back from the changes that you want to make toward a balanced life. They may even lead to poor health!

Is there anything for which you need to forgive yourself?_____
_____
_____
_____

Is there someone to whom you need to extend forgiveness?_____
_____
_____
_____

If you are at all familiar with the Twelve Steps used in Alcoholics Anonymous and other recovery groups, you have undoubtedly read about or experienced the power of forgiveness.

The principle of forgiveness works both ways. To forgive, is to release someone ... and thereby you are released, as well. To hold resentment, unforgiveness, bitterness, or a grudge against someone is to keep yourself bound to that person and that problem.

In reality, people often don't deserve to be forgiven, but that is when we have to remind ourselves of the many times we have been forgiven, especially by God. Forgiveness becomes a guiding principle for a healthy personality—if we let it. Be a forgiving person toward yourself and others.

Prayers & Passages

Bear with each other and forgive whatever grievances you may have against one another. Forgive as the Lord forgave you.
Colossians 3:13

Lord, I recognize that I have been unforgiving toward_____ (list anyone toward whom you presently hold a grudge). Help me to let go of my bitterness, to forgive and to go on. I cannot forgive without your help. Help me, Lord.

Also, Lord, I have not forgiven myself for _____ (tell God of anything for which you cannot forgive yourself). I realize you promise to forgive me, when I confess and turn from sin (1 John 1:9). Help me, now, to forgive myself. Amen.

Please, use extra paper and take extra time if you have more forgiveness to give.

Content in every situation

Positive Thought

Anxiety does not empty tomorrow of its sorrows, but only empties today of its strength.

Charles H. Spurgeon

Practical Tip

The old saying "The grass is always greener on the other side of the fence" seems to be true no matter how much we possess. We are always wishing for something that's just out of our reach.

Don't think, however, that you must always be content with every aspect of your life. There can be some benefits to dissatisfaction. You might have been less than happy with your eating and activity habits and that dissatisfaction motivated you to pick up this book and begin to make some changes. Or you may feel that the spiritual or emotional areas of your life are lacking in depth and have set new goals that you are working toward.

However, as you strive for change and progress in your life, your goal should be contentment with what you have now and where you are today in your personal growth. Avoid falling into the trap of discontentment and unhappiness by simply *wishing* for that which you don't have. Instead, *take action* and move forward toward your goals today while being content with what each day brings.

Go back to Week 2, Day 1 and look at the values you listed as most important to you. Reminding yourself of what is most important to you can help you see things in perspective, especially when you are feeling discontented with your situation.

For each value listed, reflect on how content you are right now with that value. For example, if I listed "family" as one of my values, I might reflect on the joy that my children give me and how loved I feel by my husband. If I am feeling discontented because our neighbors are vacationing in Disney World and we can't afford to go anywhere this year, I could remind myself that we can have a great family vacation right here at home!

Relist the five values that are most important to you:
1._____
2._____
3._____
4._____
5._____

How content are you right now with each value?
1._____
2._____
3._____
4._____
5._____

Express your feelings at this time: _____
_____
_____
_____
_____
_____

Prayers & Passages

But godliness with contentment is great gain.
1 Timothy 6:6

Lord, teach me to be content with what I have and who I am right now. It is a valuable lesson I long to learn! Forgive me for always wanting more. I want to thank you for all that you have given to me. I love you.

on't worry, be happy

Positive Thought

The happiness of your life depends upon the quality of your thoughts; therefore, guard accordingly.

Marcus Antoninus

Practical Tip

I (Becky) had a friend who always told me, "Only ten percent of what you worry about ever comes to pass." Whenever I remind myself of that, especially in anxious moments, I am often put at ease.

Another thought that helps me in moments of disappointment, discouragement, or missed opportunities is to ask myself, "What is the worst that could happen?" When assessing a situation based on that question, it is rarely that my answer finds my life ruined or threatened—most often it is only inconvenienced, humbled, or redirected.

Some of us decide sooner than later that worry gains nothing, nor changes anything. In fact, it often can be a time-waster, strength-sapper, faith-reducer, and trust-destroyer.

Recently, when my feelings were hurt, I found myself fretting instead of praying. I was angry. And that led to more hurt feelings—and the need for confession.

After a tearful time of sharing, I realized that fretting and worry do not bring resolution; but prayer, thinking the best of another, and speaking the truth in love will.

Instead of worrying, write a prayer expressing any fears or anxieties you might be experiencing today: _____

_____

_____

_____

_____

_____

_____

_____

_____

_____

_____

_____

Prayers & Passages

Do not fret…

Psalm 37:1

Do not be anxious about anything, but in everything, by prayer and petition, with thanksgiving, present your requests to God.

Philippians 4:6

I worry. I fret. I have manipulated. I have not trusted. Forgive me. Change me. Help me not to worry, but to pray about everything! Thank you, Lord.

Thank God!

Positive Thought

If anyone would tell you the shortest, surest way to happiness and all perfection, he must tell you to make it a rule to yourself to thank and praise God for everything that happens to you. For it is certain that whatever seeming calamity happens to you, if you thank and praise God for it, you turn it into a blessing.

William Law

Practical Tip

Everyone says, "Thank God," but do they mean...

* "Whew, I'm glad that's over."
* "What a relief!" or
* "Thank you, God!"

Thanking God in all situations makes for a very positive and practical—and perhaps radical—outlook on life!

To think about God as someone who cares and listens and shows his love to us, rather than just a figurehead of religion, is to look at life with a whole new perspective!

To thank God even when we don't understand, can't see the whole picture, or aren't feeling good about a situation is never easy, and certainly takes extra effort on our part.

Andrea, a friend of mine [Becky], shared how she struggled with her emotions as she watched her daughter, Heather, go through a difficult time in her life. Before summer began, Heather had a good group of friends from her junior high. But once summer came, distance grew between them.

Even though it was difficult, Andrea and Heather decided to thank God, trusting that he would bring something good out of this situation. And as the summer progressed, good things *did* happen. Heather began to hang out with the youth group at church. She went to Bible studies, beach parties, and even on a campout. What had started out as a dreary, lonely summer turned into what Heather described as her "best summer ever!"

To thank God in all things is not to be naive, but to trust that God is a good God who sees our struggles, sometimes disciplines us, and often rewards us. Thank God!

Write a "thank-you note" today to God for something he has done for you.

_____

_____

_____

_____

_____

_____

_____

_____

_____

_____

_____

_____

_____

Prayers & Passages

Be joyful always; pray continually; give thanks in all circumstances, for this is God's will for you in Christ Jesus.

1 Thessalonians 5:16–18

Lord, I get stubborn, impatient, even lazy sometimes. Thank you that tough times don't last forever. Thank you for being someone I can count on to watch over me and care for me. Forgive me if I've been ungrateful or complained. Thank you... in all things, thank you.

Follow your dreams

Positive Thought

We grow great by dreams. All big successes are big dreamers. They see things in the red fire of a long winter's evening, or through the mist of a rainy day. Some of us let these great dreams die, but others nourish and protect them, nurse them through the bad days 'til they bring them to the sunshine and light, which comes always to those who sincerely believe that their dreams will come true.

Woodrow Wilson

Practical Tip

A true dream never goes away. It comes back to your heart, mind, and thoughts over and over and over. A dream has the power to make you believe you can attempt the impossible, improbable, or impractical! Look at some well-known dreamers like:

❖ Gale Devers, who dreamed of competing in the Olympics and persevered through Graves Disease, recuperated, trained, and against all odds won the women's 100-yard dash in the 1992 Olympics.

❖ Abraham Lincoln, who lost many elections before becoming one of the most influential presidents of the United States.

❖ Elizabeth Dole, who as a politician and director of the Red Cross has been an exceptional role model for women to pursue their goals and dreams.

A dream list doesn't have to be a "wish" list—it can be a "do" list. I [Becky] personally have seen many dreams come true—yet other dreams remain on my list, reminding me they have yet to come true.

List any dreams that don't go away.

_____

_____

_____

_____

_____

_____

Evaluate each dream to see if it would truly fit into your lifestyle, your beliefs, and your values:

_____

_____

_____

_____

_____

_____

Now, list some ways you could make that dream become a reality.

_____

_____

_____

_____

_____

_____

Remember, a dream becomes reality when you make it a goal—and pursue it to the end!

In the morning, O LORD, you hear my voice; in the morning I lay my requests before you and wait in expectation.

Psalm 5:3

Lord, I have so many dreams—some need to be dusted off and revived, others need to be released to fly. Help me fulfill the dreams you have put into my heart. Amen.

Pursuing Hope

❖ ❖
❖ ❖
❖ ❖

This week you will continue the inward journey of making an emotional lifestyle change. Progress in the area of emotional growth may be slower than in the other areas. Don't get discouraged. You will find tools that will encourage you to track your progress, to break through barriers, and to devote yourself to finding and achieving balance. Hold on!

Admit, ask for, and accept help

Positive Thought

God can make you anything you want to be, but you have to put everything in his hands.

Mahalia Jackson

Practical Tip

To free themselves from addiction, codependency, depression, anorexia, or overeating, millions of Americans have worked through the Twelve Steps on their road to recovery. The Twelve Steps were developed by Alcoholics Anonymous. With their permission, we have rewritten them slightly and listed Bible verses to show their Christian underpinnings. Use the Twelve Steps to guide you in your journey to emotional wholeness and balance.

Step 1   We admit that we cannot handle our struggles alone. Apart from God we are powerless, and our struggles are unmanageable (John 15:5).

Step 2   We come to believe that we need Jesus Christ to restore us (Philippians 4:13).

Step 3   We make a decision to invite Jesus to come into our lives (Romans 10:9).

Step 4   We take a relentless, detailed, written, moral inventory of our lives (Psalm 139:23).

Step 5	We admit the exact nature of our wrongs to God, ourselves, and another person, and we ask for forgiveness (James 5:16).
Step 6	We are ready to let God help us change any areas we need to change (Lamentations 3:40).
Step 7	We humbly ask God to change both our attitudes and our actions (Psalm 143:10).
Step 8	We make a list of everyone we have hurt or who has hurt us and become willing to forgive or reconcile the relationship (Matthew 6:12).
Step 9	We ask forgiveness from the people we have hurt and attempt to be reconciled except if doing so would injure ourselves, them, or others (Matthew 5:23–24).
Step 10	We continue to keep a relentless, detailed, written, moral inventory of ourselves and ask for forgiveness from God as soon as we have done wrong (Proverbs 28:13).
Step 11	We continue to develop our relationship with Jesus Christ through reading our Bible, praying, and asking for his power to do his will (Philippians 2:13).
Step 12	Having been renewed by God's Spirit, we carry this message of hope to others and demonstrate what we have learned in all our affairs (2 Corinthians 5:18–19).

If you are interested in more information on the Twelve Steps or Twelve-Step Groups, see the listing in the back of this devotional.

Prayers & Passages

I am the vine; you are the branches. If a man remains in me and I in him, he will bear much fruit; apart from me you can do nothing.

John 15:5

Lord, I admit that I need help with:_____

_____
_____
_____
_____
_____
_____
_____
_____
_____
_____
_____
_____
_____
_____
_____
_____

I ask you to help me. Show me the steps I can take to continue my healing process. Thank you. Amen.

ile markers

Positive Thought

Remember your past mis-takes just long enough to profit by them.

Dan McKinnon

Practical Tip ✦

Progress in the area of emotional growth may be slower for you than your progress in the physical, mental, and spiritual areas of your life. When you don't see measurable progress immediately, you may be tempted to give up on your goals. That's why tracking your progress in different ways is an effective way to stay motivated as well as accountable to your goals.

As a reminder, go back to Week 1, Day 6 and review the 90-day emotional goals that you set for yourself. Relist them below:

90-day emotional goals _____

_____

_____

_____

The following four "mile markers" allow you to gauge your emotional growth. For each of your 90-day emotional goals, measure your progress using any or all of these tools.

1. Ask a close friend or spouse how you are

doing. A person who is very close to you and who may be familiar with your efforts and struggles can give you a good update on your progress. Many of the emotional problems we are struggling to change are most evident to our families or those who spend the most time with us. Validation from those sources—that they see change in you—is valuable and will give you hope to continue. For example, when your child tells you that you don't yell at him or her as often, you will know you are truly making progress and achieving your goals.

2. Ask others around you how you are doing. Co-workers, friends, and neighbors can also give you a progress report. For example, ask your secretary if you are making progress with your habit of procrastination. If she tells you that you throw everything on her desk at the last minute, your perception of your progress may receive a reality check!

3. Track your progress in a journal. Daily or weekly journaling will keep you accountable to yourself and allow you to go back periodically to see how far you've come. Writing down your thoughts, feelings, struggles, and triumphs in itself can be a tool for emotional growth as well as a yardstick to measure progress.

4. Measure yourself by God's Word. The Bible is like a plumb line, giving you a frame of reference to keep you on track. God's Word gives specific instructions to avoid worry, anger, jealousy, and other emotions that can threaten to rule our lives. Use the Word to measure and study your progress by reading and following God's instructions for your life. Look up verses in the Bible that deal with the specific areas you struggle with and use them as a gauge or compass, moving you in the direction of God's Word.

reaking through

Positive Thought

It's not what you are that holds you back, it's what you think you're not.

Dennis Waitley

Practical Tip

By now, in your 90-day journey, you have broken through various barriers, struggled over rough spots, and persevered until you saw or made a change.

Some of you may have set a goal to work out at a gym three times a week, but experienced a few unexpected scheduling conflicts. Instead of doing nothing, you decided to work out at the gym once a week and ride your stationary bike two mornings before work. Great thinking! Others of you may have really got the hang of counting fat grams and are not only eating differently, but enjoying it.

List any areas where you have made a breakthrough:_____

_____

_____

_____

_____

_____

_____

In any situation that involves change, you will be faced with mountains, obstacles, road blocks, fences, and ravines. You may have to go over, under, around, or through—but you can break through with persistence, patience, prayer, and positive affirmations.

For example, you may have set a goal to lose a certain amount of weight or number of inches and have only reached the halfway mark. Be encouraged by the progress you've made so far! Don't give up now, but persevere.

List any areas where you still need to make a breakthrough: _____
_____
_____
_____
_____
_____

What are some of the steps you can take or attitudes you can change to help you break through? _____
_____
_____
_____
_____
_____
_____

Learning to see your failures as common rather than catastrophic will give you courage to move forward and break through the barriers.

Prayers & Passages

Blessed is the man who perseveres under trial, because when he has stood the test, he will receive the crown of life that God has promised to those who love him.

James 1:12

Lord, give me new ideas, fresh courage, and the hope I need to keep on persevering in my daily struggles. I need your help to

_____
_____
_____
_____
_____
_____
_____
_____

Amen.

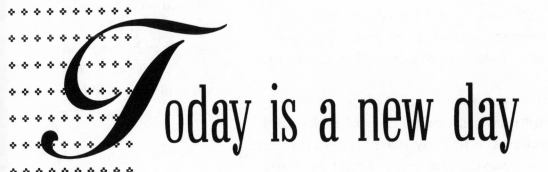

Today is a new day

Positive Thought

If a door slams shut it means that God is pointing to an open door further on down.

Anna Delaney Peale
(1875–1939)

Practical Tip

No matter how determined we are, we'll all experience a setback. Perhaps ...

❖ Yesterday you went to a birthday party and chipped and dipped and M&M'd it to excess, and now you're feeling guilty.

❖ Last week you forgot your mother-in-law's birthday and ended up fighting with your husband over whose responsibility it was to remember.

❖ You've said "yes" one too many times to PTA, Scouts, and committee meetings and haven't had your quiet time for days.

One gift you are given when you wake up each morning is a new day. A new day in which to make healthy choices, dwell on what is good and right, and allow God to work in your life.

Don't be discouraged with yesterday. Don't let the past failures sap your strength. And don't get down on yourself. Don't look back—but look up!

Try this: Rather than feeling guilty about that birthday party, get active and start eating healthy foods again.

✤ Instead of harboring anger any longer toward your husband, buy a belated birthday card and add a humorous note.

✤ Don't try to catch up on your quiet time, but start where you left off.

Today I will_____

_____

_____

Today I want to_____

_____

Today I look forward to_____

_____

_____

Today I will start_____

_____

Today I will call_____

_____

_____

Today I will take_____

_____

_____

Today I will try_____

_____

_____

Today I can_____

_____

_____

Remember, you've been given a brand new day—a whole new start—by a great, good God!

Because of the LORD's great love we are not consumed, for his compassions never fail. They are new every morning; great is your faithfulness.

Lamentations 3:22–23

Lord, thank you that today is a new day. Please give me a fresh start and a positive attitude as I walk through this day—hand in hand with you. Amen.

Hope... holds on!

Positive Thought

Hold
On,
Pray
Expectantly!
Robert Schuller

Practical Tip

Hope is defined as desire accompanied by confident expectation. That desire and expectation can keep you moving forward when everything else seems to be pushing you back. Do you look toward your future with hope and anticipation or with fear and trepidation? Faith, hope, and trust in God and the abilities he has given you can carry you through tough times and big changes.

Hope gives you the courage to take the direction that you really want to take. If you believe that you can get on an exercise program and stay on it for the rest of your life, you are far more likely to succeed than if you doubt your ability to make and keep that commitment.

Change is an inevitable part of life, and when you have hope to hold on to, change becomes less intimidating. Hope helps you to make changes in your life when you are afraid. If you are overweight, you may fear changing your unhealthy eating habits because of the changes that weight loss may bring. Hope gives you courage to believe that you can become a changed person, giving you the strength to pursue a healthy diet.

What do you need hope for today?_____
_____
_____
_____
_____

Hope looks for a second chance.

Hope anticipates the future.

Hope gains momentum through prayer.

Hope lifts you when you are low.

Hope looks for the positive in all situations.

Hope anchors itself in God.

Hope doesn't give up.

Prayers & Passages

Why are you downcast, O my soul? Why so disturbed within me? Put your hope in God, for I will yet praise him, my Savior and my God.

Psalm 42:5

When I put my hope in you and in your written word, I can't help but be encouraged. Lift me, Lord. Help me. Be near to me today. Give me hope that's heaven-sent. Give me hope throughout my day. Amen.

ully devoted

Positive Thought

Every golden era in human history proceeds from the devotion and righteous passion of some single individual. There are not bona fide mass movements; it just looks that way. There is always one man who knows his God and knows where he is going.

Richard E. Day

Practical Tip

An athlete, in his or her pursuit of world-class excellence, trains for hours each day. Achieving the strength, endurance, and skill that it takes to be the best requires weeks and years of constant practice. With the same fervor, a scholar seeking wisdom spends hours reading and studying in pursuit of knowledge. This devotion leads both athlete and scholar to excellence in their respective areas.

That same dedication to pursue a balanced lifestyle can lead you to a level of excellence in your goals, as well. Balance between your inner self and your outer self doesn't mean comparing or competing with others. As you devote yourself to finding and achieving your set goals, both you and those around you will see excellence as a trademark of your life.

Elton Trueblood reminds us, "Discipline is the price of freedom. Excellence comes at a price."

Devote yourself to physical balance. Getting and keeping your body healthy will give you the physical strength to move forward and make change.

Physical health and energy make growth in other areas of your life possible as well.

Devote yourself to mental balance. Stimulating your mind and continuing your education will give you increased wisdom and knowledge of life. Learning teaches humility as we realize how much there is to know.

Devote yourself to emotional balance. Understanding yourself, accepting yourself for who you are, learning to love yourself, and working on handling your emotional strengths and struggles can give you a stronger character to draw upon in every crisis you face.

Devote yourself to spiritual balance. Daily prayer invites God to be involved in your actions and decisions. If you face each day with God's strength and wisdom, the impossible turns possible!

It should have come as no surprise to me, but when I [Becky] finally decided to prioritize my spiritual growth, only then did my life-long struggle with weight control become manageable. Once I had learned to discipline the spiritual area of my life, the physical, emotional, and mental areas of my life came together.

This is a trustworthy saying. And I want you to stress these things, so that those who have trusted in God may be careful to devote themselves to doing what is good. These things are excellent and profitable for everyone.

Titus 3:8

Lord, I always believed that you have something for me to do in my life that will make a difference in my world. Please give me the desire to devote myself to excellence in the physical, mental, emotional, and spiritual areas of my life, so that I will be ready whenever you call. Amen.

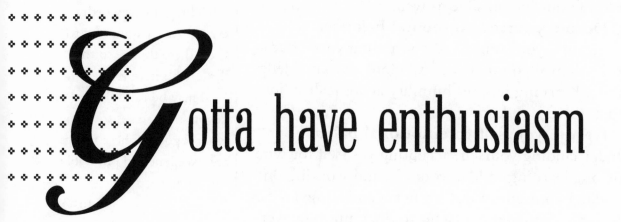

Gotta have enthusiasm

Positive Thought

Every tomorrow has two handles. You can take hold of the handle of anxiety or the handle of enthusiasm. Upon your choice so will be the day.

Anonymous

Practical Tip

Enthusiasm. Exuberance. Energy. Exhilaration.

These are the qualities that will bring new life into an old chore. They bring humor and joy into a silent, stuffy situation. They won't let you make excuses, drag your feet, or be sedentary!

Even as I wrote about enthusiasm, I wondered if it really worked. Could I fight fatigue simply with enthusiasm?

I [Becky] gave myself the perfect test. I usually bike ride in the morning, but my riding partner was ill, so I hadn't exercised yet. I don't like to bike ride alone. I never go in the late afternoon because it's hot, I have to make dinner, and I'm out of energy by then.

But I took a closer look at today's quote and began to talk to myself: "You could really benefit from this workout physically because you are going out of town. You need to work off the stress of writing deadlines. And you'll have accomplished something you've never done!"

By that point, I actually had gotten excited—so I took off on a forty-five minute bike ride. It works! People with enthusiasm ...

- create excitement,
- expect fun, and
- look for surprises.

Did you know that enthusiasm is not so much an outward characteristic, but an inward quality? The Greek derivative of enthusiasm is entheos, meaning "in God" or "God within"!

What a quality to cultivate in your own life—God within you, giving life, love, and laughter!

Who is someone that you consider enthusiastic?____

_____

_____

Do you consider yourself enthusiastic?_____

_____

_____

What area of your life most needs enthusiasm right now?_____

_____

_____

_____

_____

_____

Prayers & Passages

Now to him who is able to do immeasurably more than all we ask or imagine, according to his power that is at work within us.

Ephesians 3:20

Lord, create in me enthusiasm for all that you want to do in and through my life. Go beyond what I could even imagine! I love you. Amen.

Peace

❖ ❖

❖ ❖

❖ ❖

Peace for the journey is possible. Just because your 90-day journey is coming to a close does not mean you should cease making progress. As you press on toward your goals of a healthy mind, body, and spirit, you will undoubtedly experience a heart at peace. Remember, lasting peace for your life-long journey comes one day at time. Press on!

Congratulations!

Positive Thought

Face your deficiencies and acknowledge them; but do not let them master you. Let them teach you patience, sweetness, insight.... When we do the best we can, we never know what miracle is wrought in our life, or in the life of another.

Helen Keller

Practical Tip

Take a moment and congratulate yourself on the progress that you've made in balancing your life. Progress, whether you do it "slowly and steadily" or in "leaps and bounds," will keep your life dynamic. A dynamic life is one that is in motion, active, and filled with change.

It is not only important to periodically evaluate your progress in individual areas of your life, but to balance each of these areas, as well. If you remember, in Week 2, Day 5 we used a chart to determine which areas of your life were in balance, and which areas were out of balance or needed improvement. Let's look at that chart again. Now, eleven weeks later, put a check under the heading that most accurately reflects how you are doing at spending time growing in each area of your life.

Balanced Life Areas	Struggling	OK	Improving	Strong
Spiritual Life	❏	❏	❏	❏
Fitness/Activity	❏	❏	❏	❏
Healthful Eating/Nutrition	❏	❏	❏	❏
Mental/Professional Growth	❏	❏	❏	❏
Personal Time	❏	❏	❏	❏
Family Time	❏	❏	❏	❏
Social Relationships	❏	❏	❏	❏
Church Activities	❏	❏	❏	❏
Community Activities	❏	❏	❏	❏

Compare today's chart with your chart from Week 2. Do you see progress in the areas that you felt needed change? How well balanced are you in each of the lifestyle areas? _____

_____

_____

_____

_____

In order to continue making progress, it is important to regularly reassess the balance in each individual area, as well as review your total picture every few months. Charting progress will motivate you to continue your pursuit for balance!

Prayers & Passages

May the God of hope fill you with all joy and peace as you trust in him, so that you may overflow with hope by the power of the Holy Spirit.

Romans 15:13

Lord, I'm overflowing with the hope that through this journey I have moved toward a balanced, more active life while growing spiritually, emotionally, and mentally. Grant me an extra measure of your Holy Spirit, Lord, as I continue on.

Pursuing excellence, not perfection

Positive Thought

Aim for success, not perfection. Never give up your right to be wrong, because then you will lose the ability to learn new things and to move forward with your life. Remember that fear always lurks behind perfectionism.... Confronting your fears and allowing yourself the right to be human can, paradoxically, make you a far happier and more productive person.

Dr. David M. Burns

Practical Tip

The mere thought of striving for excellence each day can be discouraging if you think of excellence as just one more big responsibility in an already full day. Many times when we think of excellence we equate it with perfection. Perfection is elusive, and the pursuit of it can cause frustration and dissatisfaction in every area of your life.

Here's an example: I [Candice] am trying to be a perfect mother. Then I have one of those days when all I do is change diapers, settle sibling fights, and clean up messes. By the end of the day I am snapping at both my husband and the children. As I lay in bed that night I feel like a failure as a mother and know that I'll never achieve the perfection I seek.

If I strive for excellence instead, my goals as a mother will include loving unconditionally, being a guiding force and role model, and meeting all of my children's needs. I will still have those trying days, but at the end of the day I can reflect on my efforts of pushing on toward and achieving my goals.

Pressing on toward your goals creates excellence in your life. Look at each day as an opportunity to press ahead, to grow and to change.

Are there areas in your life where you are striving for perfection and finding it elusive? _____
_____
_____
_____

How can you change your thinking and strive for excellence instead? _____
_____
_____
_____

Write a personal prayer to God, expressing your thoughts and feelings at this time ... _____
_____
_____
_____
_____
_____
_____
_____
_____
_____

Lean on me

Positive Thought

Anxiety is the natural result when our hopes are centered on anything short of God and his will for us.

Billy Graham

Practical Tip

At the end of any given day, if you were to take an "Attitude/Action Check," which words would most often describe you?

peaceful or anxious
calm or angry
active or idle
happy or sad
encouraged or depressed
disciplined or lazy
motivated or lethargic
kind or rude
faithful or fickle
generous or selfish
humble or arrogant
timely or late
patient or impatient

This little "check" is not meant to discourage you, but to encourage you to be aware of your attitudes and actions on a regular basis.

When I [Becky] look over this list, I see quite a few areas that need improvement. Although that is hard to admit, I've found it helpful to humble myself before God and ask for his help to change. And I can come to him willingly, without fear, because I know that he is interested in strengthening me in my areas of weakness.

If you could choose one area on this list to ask God to help you with, what would it be?_____

_____

_____

_____

_____

_____

_____

Prayers & Passages

Humble yourselves before the Lord, and he will lift you up.

James 4:10

Lord, I do need to lean on you more. I want to be more patient and kind, more motivated, more generous ... help me.

I am so grateful to be able to talk to you, to admit my weaknesses, and to find your forgiveness. I humble myself before you and I ask that you would lift me up. Amen.

A heart at peace
gives life to the body

Positive Thought

Serenity comes not alone by removing the outward causes and occasions of fear, but by the discovery of inward reservoirs to draw upon.

Rufus M. Jones

Practical Tip

Throughout your 90-day journey you have worked at overcoming physical challenges by drawing upon your inner resources of courage, determination, faith, perseverance, hope, discipline, sacrifice, and patience.

You have undoubtedly discovered some very interesting characteristics about yourself on this journey.

If your successes have been abundant in any area, share your "excited" feelings at this time: _____

_____

_____

_____

If you have more struggles in certain areas, share your "honest" feelings at this time: _____

_____

_____

_____

As you look back over this 90-day journey of making lifestyle changes, what encouraging words do you have for yourself? _____
_____
_____
_____
_____
_____
_____
_____

Prayers & Passages

Now may the Lord of peace himself give you peace at all times and in every way. The Lord be with all of you.

2 Thessalonians 3:16

Lord, please fill my heart with a peace that comes from you, a peace that overcomes my fears, overshadows my obstacles, and increases my courage. Thank you.

Fit, filled, and on fire

Positive Thought

*Enthusiasm is a kind of
faith that has been set afire.*
George Matthew Adams
(1878–1962)

Practical Tip

Total fitness means a healthy body, mind, and spirit. The only way to achieve this balance and feel "fit" is to take action and spend time exercising your inner and outer person.

What would happen if you joined a health club, went every day, and just sat and watched other people exercise? Nothing! The best intentions in the world will not create change in your life. Goal-setting is a good first step, but will not produce change if you don't take action. To achieve a fit body, you need to be active on a regular basis. Activity that strengthens your cardiovascular system and your muscles, combined with stretching and relaxation exercises, will improve your physical fitness.

In the same way you need to strengthen your inner person with mental, spiritual, and emotional exercises.

As you ...
+ **"Exercise"** in prayer, you develop spiritual

fitness. Time spent in the Word increases your faith, which in turn increases your spiritual strength.

✧ **"Work out"** mentally, you will challenge yourself to learn new things. Mental growth will stretch your mind and allow for continued growth.

✧ **"Exert"** yourself, you will find the time for your emotional development. Be at peace with your feelings of who you are and where your life is at today, and you'll discover more potential than you ever imagined!

Prayers & Passages

Now faith is being sure of what we hope for and certain of what we do not see.

Hebrews 11:1

Lord, as this 90-day journey comes to a close, I realize my whole life is a journey to be traveled. Give me the desire to be active, to exercise my faith, to stretch my mind, and to exert myself to grow emotionally. Help me to grow in faith—to believe what I cannot see, but to know that you have great things waiting for me. Thank you.

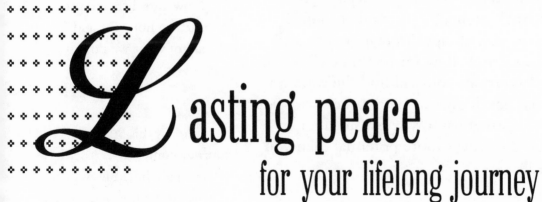

Lasting peace
for your lifelong journey

Positive Thought

It is impossible to have the feeling of peace and serenity without being at rest with God.

Dorothy H. Pentecost

Practical Tip

Peace gives...

Patience to the mind,
Energy to the body,
Assurance to the heart,
Comfort to the soul,
Endurance for life's long journey.

As you review the last 90 Days...
1. Have you gained patience in any area? Explain:

_____
_____
_____
_____
_____

2. Have your energy and activity levels increased? Describe: _____

_____
_____
_____

3. Have you been assured of God's concern and care for you throughout this journey? Give an example:

_____

_____

_____

_____

4. What has been a source of comfort to you during this journey? Be specific: _____

_____

_____

_____

_____

5. What are your plans to continue in your pursuit of a balanced life?

Physical _____

_____

Mental_____

_____

Emotional_____

_____

Spiritual_____

_____

Prayers & Passages

Peace I leave with you; my peace I give you. I do not give to you as the world gives. Do not let your hearts be troubled and do not be afraid.

John 14:27

Lord, give me a peace that goes beyond my under-standing—a quiet calm, a comforting presence that overcomes my anxieties and fears. Grant me the patience I need to carry out the goals I have set for myself, the energy to keep active through each season of my life, the assurance in my heart that you are as close as a prayer, the comfort that comes from your word and your Spirit... and Lord, grant me the endurance to make continuous progress throughout my lifelong journey. Amen.